Praise for Qiskit Pocket Guide

Qiskit Pocket Guide is a convenient, compact Qiskit reference book for quantum programming all in one place.

—*Jay Gambetta, IBM Fellow and VP of IBM Quantum*

This pocket guide is an excellent overview of core Qiskit functionality with a concise, yet practical, code-first approach.

—*Abby Mitchell, Quantum Developer Advocate*

Learning quantum computing can be daunting, and remembering all the functionality in the Qiskit API can be equally so. This book provides a necessary companion for coders who want to take full advantage of the power and elegant features provided by Qiskit.

—*Dr. Bob Sutor, Quantum industry expert and author,* Dancing with Qubits *and* Dancing with Python

This is an incredibly handy book–for beginners and advanced users alike–that describes the many functionalities and features of Qiskit, organized in a clear and intuitive way. I expect it is unlikely to find its way off my desk and into a bookshelf any time soon.

—*Dr. John Watrous,*
Technical Director, IBM
Quantum Education

Concise yet extensive, this belongs in the pocket of every Qiskit developer.

—*Lia Yeh,*
CS PhD student,
Quantum Group,
University of Oxford

Very crisp and clear book for quantum developers of all levels!

—*Robert Loredo, IBM*
Quantum Ambassador
Worldwide Lead

A clear and well-organized reference; readers exploring quantum programming will enjoy simple and specific steps to get QPU programs up and running, while even experienced Qiskit users may discover some surprising features.

—*Eric R. Johnston,*
coauthor of Programming
Quantum Computers

Qiskit Pocket Guide
Quantum Development with Qiskit

James L. Weaver and Frank J. Harkins

Beijing · Boston · Farnham · Sebastopol · Tokyo   O'REILLY®

Qiskit Pocket Guide

by James L. Weaver and Frank J. Harkins

Published by O'Reilly Media, Inc., 1005 Gravenstein Highway North, Sebastopol, CA 95472.

O'Reilly books may be purchased for educational, business, or sales promotional use. Online editions are also available for most titles (*http://oreilly.com*). For more information, contact our corporate/institutional sales department: 800-998-9938 or *corporate@oreilly.com*.

Acquisitions Editor: Suzanne McQuade
Development Editor: Shira Evans
Production Editor: Katherine Tozer
Copyeditor: Piper Editorial Consulting, LLC
Proofreader: Tom Sullivan
Indexer: nSight, Inc.
Interior Designer: David Futato
Cover Designer: Karen Montgomery
Illustrator: Kate Dullea

July 2022:   First Edition

Revision History for the First Release

         2022-06-15:   First Release

See *https://oreil.ly/qkpgERR* for release details.

978-1-098-11247-9

[LSI]

Table of Contents

Preface

Qiskit is an open source SDK (software development kit) for working with quantum computers at the level of pulses, circuits, and application modules. The purpose of this book is to provide a succinct guide for developers to use while creating applications that leverage quantum computers and simulators.

We hope this book will enable developers to actively participate in the open source Qiskit community. The Qiskit community, as well as documentation, tutorials, and other resources, is available at Qiskit (*https://qiskit.org*).

How This Book Is Structured

Our goal in this guide is to address much of the functionality of Qiskit that application developers will routinely use. Some of this Qiskit functionality is considered to be fundamental to quantum computing. Other Qiskit functionality supports quantum computing concepts such as quantum information and quantum algorithms. Qiskit has additional functionality that we've deemed essential for quantum application development. We've structured the book at a high level according to the aforementioned functionality, with individual chapters drilling into the specifics. The chapters are divided into three parts:

Part I, Qiskit Fundamentals

In the first part of the book, we show you how to use Qiskit to create quantum circuits. Quantum circuits contain instructions and gates, so we discuss how to use the ones provided in Qiskit, as well as how to create your own. We then show you how to run quantum circuits on quantum computers and simulators and demonstrate how to visualize results. To round out Part I, we discuss the *transpiler* and how it converts a quantum circuit into instructions that run on a target quantum computer or simulator.

Part II, Quantum Information and Algorithms

In the second part of this book, we discuss Qiskit modules responsible for implementing quantum information concepts (specifically states, operators, channels, and measures). We also present facilities in Qiskit that implement quantum algorithms, as well as a facility known in Qiskit as *operator flow*. A developer may use some of the functionality in Part II to develop quantum applications at higher levels of abstraction than quantum circuits.

Part III, Additional Essential Functionality

In the third and final part of this book, we cover essential Qiskit functionality, some of which drills into information already discussed and some of which is newly presented. Specifically, we explore the *standard operations* of the Qiskit circuit library, and new ground is uncovered when we discuss how to work with quantum providers and backends. In addition, we'll introduce QASM 3.0 and demonstrate how to create quantum programs with this quantum assembly language.

Conventions Used in This Book

The following typographical conventions are used in this book:

Italic

Indicates new terms, URLs, email addresses, filenames, and file extensions.

```
Constant width
```
Used for program listings, as well as within paragraphs to refer to program elements such as variable or function names, databases, data types, environment variables, statements, and keywords.

NOTE

This element signifies a general note.

Using Code Examples

Supplemental material (code examples, exercises, etc.) is available for download at *https://github.com/qiskit-community/qiskit-pocket-guide#readme*.

If you have a technical question or a problem using the code examples, please send email to *bookquestions@oreilly.com*.

This book is here to help you get your job done. In general, if example code is offered with this book, you may use it in your programs and documentation. You do not need to contact us for permission unless you're reproducing a significant portion of the code. For example, writing a program that uses several chunks of code from this book does not require permission. Selling or distributing examples from O'Reilly books does require permission. Answering a question by citing this book and quoting example code does not require permission. Incorporating a significant amount of example code from this book into your product's documentation does require permission.

We appreciate, but generally do not require, attribution. An attribution usually includes the title, author, publisher, and ISBN. For example: "*Qiskit Pocket Guide* by James L. Weaver and Frank J. Harkins (O'Reilly). Copyright 2022 James Weaver and Frank Harkins, 978-1-098-11247-9."

If you feel that your use of code examples falls outside fair use or the permission given above, feel free to contact us at *permissions@oreilly.com*.

O'Reilly Online Learning

 For more than 40 years, *O'Reilly Media* has provided technology and business training, knowledge, and insight to help companies succeed.

Our unique network of experts and innovators share their knowledge and expertise through books, articles, and our online learning platform. O'Reilly's online learning platform gives you on-demand access to live training courses, in-depth learning paths, interactive coding environments, and a vast collection of text and video from O'Reilly and 200+ other publishers. For more information, visit *http://oreilly.com*.

How to Contact Us

Please address comments and questions concerning this book to the publisher:

O'Reilly Media, Inc.
1005 Gravenstein Highway North
Sebastopol, CA 95472
800-998-9938 (in the United States or Canada)
707-829-0515 (international or local)
707-829-0104 (fax)

We have a web page for this book, where we list errata, examples, and any additional information. You can access this page at *https://oreil.ly/qiskit-pocket-guide*.

Email *bookquestions@oreilly.com* to comment or ask technical questions about this book.

For news and information about our books and courses, visit *https://oreilly.com*.

Find us on LinkedIn: *https://linkedin.com/company/oreilly-media*.

Follow us on Twitter: *https://twitter.com/oreillymedia*.

Watch us on YouTube: *https://www.youtube.com/oreillymedia*.

Acknowledgments

This book would not have been possible without a supporting team of innovative people at IBM Quantum and in the larger quantum computing community. The authors would like to thank the amazing O'Reilly team, including Kristen Brown, Danny Elfanbaum, Shira Evans, Zan McQuade, Jonathon Owen, Kim Sandoval, and Katherine Tozer. The authors also appreciate the invaluable contributions made by technical reviewers Luciano Bello, Nick Bronn, Barry Burd, Junye Huang, Eric Johnston, Robert Loredo, and Iskandar Sitdikov.

James Weaver would like to thank Julie, Lori, Kelli, Kaleb, Jillian, Levi, and Oliver for their understanding and encouragement while working on this book. As a lifelong classical developer, James is also thankful that quantum mechanical phenomena baked into nature may potentially be leveraged to solve problems not possible with classical computers. "The heavens declare the glory of God, and the sky above proclaims his handiwork" (Psalm 19:1).

Frank Harkins would like to thank the Qiskit team for all their great work on Qiskit and its documentation and for answering all his questions. Frank would also like to thank Rose, Matt, Joanne, Keith, Libby, and Martha for their constant support over the course of writing this book.

PART I
Qiskit Fundamentals

If one has left this entire system to itself for an hour, one would say that the cat still lives if meanwhile no atom has decayed. The psi-function of the entire system would express this by having in it the living and dead cat (pardon the expression) mixed or smeared out in equal parts.

—Erwin Schrödinger

Underlying all programs developed using Qiskit are some fundamental concepts and modules. In the first part of this book, we'll explore these fundamentals, beginning with Chapter 1, "Quantum Circuits and Operations". In that chapter, we'll demonstrate how to create quantum circuits, populate them with commonly used gates and instructions, obtain information about quantum circuits, and manipulate them.

In Chapter 2, "Running Quantum Circuits", we'll demonstrate how to use Qiskit classes and functions to run quantum circuits on quantum simulators and devices. We'll also show you how to monitor the status of a job, as well as how to obtain its results. Then in Chapter 3, "Visualizing Quantum Measurements and States", we'll show you how to leverage graphical features of Qiskit to visualize quantum states and results.

Finally in Chapter 4, "Using the Transpiler", we'll discuss the process of *transpilation* in which the operations of a quantum circuit are converted into instructions for running on a particular quantum simulator or device.

## CHAPTER 1

Quantum Circuits and Operations

In Qiskit, quantum programs are normally expressed with quantum circuits that contain quantum operations. Quantum circuits are represented by the `QuantumCircuit` class, and quantum operations are represented by subclasses of the class `Instruction`.

Constructing Quantum Circuits

A quantum circuit may be created by supplying an argument that indicates the number of desired quantum wires (qubits) for that circuit. This is often supplied as an integer:

```
from qiskit import QuantumCircuit
QuantumCircuit(2)
```

Optionally, the number of desired classical wires (bits) may also be specified. The first argument refers to the number of quantum wires, and the second argument the number of classical wires:

```
QuantumCircuit(2, 2)
```

The number of desired quantum and classical wires may also be expressed by supplying instances of `QuantumRegister` and `ClassicalRegister` as arguments to `QuantumCircuit`. These classes are addressed in "Using the QuantumRegister Class" on page 24 and "Using the ClassicalRegister Class" on page 25.

Using the QuantumCircuit Class

The QuantumCircuit class contains a large number of methods and attributes. The purpose of many of its methods is to apply quantum operations to a quantum circuit. Most of its other methods and attributes either manipulate or report information about a quantum circuit.

Commonly used gates

Table 1-1 contains some commonly used single-qubit gates and code examples. The variable qc refers to an instance of QuantumCircuit that contains at least four quantum wires.

Table 1-1. Commonly used single-qubit gates in Qiskit

Names	Example	Notes
H, Hadamard	qc.h(0)	Applies H gate to qubit 0. See "HGate" on page 153.
I, Identity	qc.id(2) or qc.i(2)	Applies I gate to qubit 2. See "IGate" on page 153.
P, Phase	qc.p(math.pi/2,0)	Applies P gate with $\pi/2$ phase rotation to qubit 0. See "PhaseGate" on page 153.
RX	qc.rx(math.pi/4,2)	Applies RX gate with $\pi/4$ rotation to qubit 2. See "RXGate" on page 153.
RY	qc.ry(math.pi/8,0)	Applies RY gate with $\pi/8$ rotation to qubit 0. See "RYGate" on page 154.
RZ	qc.rz(math.pi/2,1)	Applies RZ gate with $\pi/2$ rotation to qubit 1. See "RZGate" on page 154.
S	qc.s(3)	Applies S gate to qubit 3. Equivalent to P gate with $\pi/2$ phase rotation. See "SGate" on page 154.

Names	Example	Notes
S†	`qc.sdg(3)`	Applies S† gate to qubit 3. Equivalent to P gate with $3\pi/2$ phase rotation. See "SdgGate" on page 155.
SX	`qc.sx(2)`	Applies SX (square root of X) gate to qubit 2. Equivalent to RX gate with $\pi/2$ rotation. See "SXGate" on page 155.
T	`qc.t(1)`	Applies T gate to qubit 1. Equivalent to P gate with $\pi/4$ phase rotation. See "TGate" on page 155.
T†	`qc.tdg(1)`	Applies T† gate to qubit 1. Equivalent to P gate with $7\pi/4$ phase rotation. See "TdgGate" on page 156.
U	`qc.u(math.pi/ 2,0,math.pi,1)`	Applies rotation with 3 Euler angles to qubit 1. See "UGate" on page 156.
X	`qc.x(3)`	Applies X gate to qubit 3. See "XGate" on page 156.
Y	`qc.y([0,2,3])`	Applies Y gates to qubits 0, 2, and 3. See "YGate" on page 156.
Z	`qc.z(2)`	Applies Z gate to qubit 2. Equivalent to P gate with π phase rotation. See "ZGate" on page 157.

Figure 1-1 contains a nonsensical circuit with all of the single-qubit gate examples from Table 1-1.

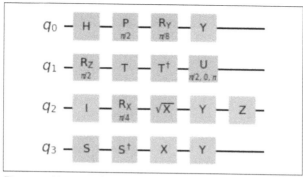

Figure 1-1. Nonsensical circuit with single-qubit gate examples

Table 1-2 contains some commonly used multiqubit gates and code examples. The variable qc refers to an instance of Quantum Circuit that contains at least four quantum wires.

Table 1-2. Commonly used multiqubit gates in Qiskit

Names	Example	Notes
CCX, Toffoli	qc.ccx(0,1,2)	Applies the X gate to quantum wire 2, subject to the state of the control qubits on wires 0 and 1. See "CCXGate" on page 158.
CH	qc.ch(0,1)	Applies the H gate to quantum wire 1, subject to the state of the control qubit on wire 0. See "CHGate" on page 159.
CP, Control-Phase	qc.cp(math.pi/4,0,1)	Applies the phase gate to quantum wire 1, subject to the state of the control qubit on wire 0. See "CPhaseGate" on page 159.
CRX, Control-RX	qc.crx(math.pi/2,2,3)	Applies the RX gate to quantum wire 3, subject to the state of the control qubit on wire 2. See "CRXGate" on page 159.

Names	Example	Notes
CRY, Control-RY	qc.cry(math.pi/8,2,3)	Applies the RY gate to quantum wire 3, subject to the state of the control qubit on wire 2. See "CRYGate" on page 160.
CRZ	qc.crz(math.pi/4,0,1)	Applies the RZ gate to quantum wire 1, subject to the state of the control qubit on wire 0. See "CRZGate" on page 160.
CSwap, Fredkin	qc.cswap(0,2,3) or qc.fredkin(0,2,3)	Swaps the qubit states of wires 2 and 3, subject to the state of the control qubit on wire 0. See "CSwapGate" on page 160.
CSX	qc.csx(0,1)	Applies the SX (square root of X) gate to quantum wire 1, subject to the state of the control qubit on wire 0. See "CSXGate" on page 160.
CU	qc.cu(math.pi/2,0,math.pi,0,0,1)	Applies the U gate with an additional global phase argument to quantum wire 1, subject to the state of the control qubit on wire 0. See "CUGate" on page 161.
CX, CNOT	qc.cx(2,3) or qc.cnot(2,3)	Applies the X gate to quantum wire 3, subject to the state of the control qubit on wire 2. See "CXGate" on page 161.
CY, Control-Y	qc.cy(2,3)	Applies the Y gate to quantum wire 3, subject to the state of the control qubit on wire 2. See "CYGate" on page 161.
CZ, Control-Z	qc.cz(1,2)	Applies the Z gate to quantum wire 2, subject to the state of the control qubit on wire 1. See "CZGate" on page 162.

Names	Example	Notes
DCX	`qc.dcx(2,3)`	Applies two CNOT gates whose control qubits are on wires 2 and 3. See "DCXGate" on page 162.
iSwap	`qc.iswap(0,1)`	Swaps the qubit states of wires 0 and 1, and changes the phase of the $|01\rangle$ and $|10\rangle$ amplitudes by i. See "iSwapGate" on page 162.
MCP, Multi-control phase	`qc.mcp(math.pi/4, [0,1,2],3)`	Applies the phase gate to quantum wire 3, subject to the state of the control qubits on wires 0, 1, and 2. See "MCPhaseGate" on page 163.
MCX, Multi-control X	`qc.mcx([0,1,2],3)`	Applies the X gate to quantum wire 3, subject to the state of the control qubits on wires 0, 1, and 2. See "MCXGate" on page 163.
Swap	`qc.swap(2,3)`	Swaps the qubit states of wires 2 and 3. See "SwapGate" on page 163.

Figure 1-2 contains a nonsensical circuit with all of the multi-qubit gate examples from Table 1-2.

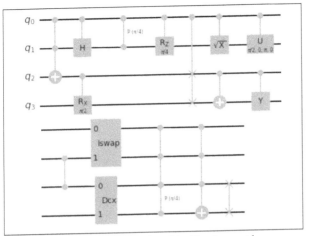

Figure 1-2. Nonsensical circuit with multiqubit gate examples

Drawing a quantum circuit

The `draw()` method draws a quantum circuit in various formats.

Using the draw() method. The following code snippet uses the `draw()` method in the default format:

```
qc = QuantumCircuit(3)
qc.h(0)
qc.cx(0, 1)
qc.cx(0, 2)
qc.draw()
```

Figure 1-3 shows the drawn circuit.

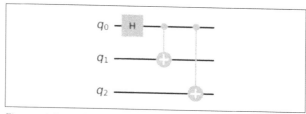

Figure 1-3. Example circuit visualization using the draw() method

Creating a barrier

The barrier() method places a *barrier* on a circuit (shown in Figure 1-4), providing both visual and functional separation between gates on a quantum circuit. Gates on either side of a barrier are not candidates for being optimized together as the circuit is converted to run on quantum hardware or a simulator.

NOTE

The set of gates expressed using Qiskit represents an abstraction for the actual gates implemented on a given quantum computer or simulator. Qiskit *transpiles* the gates into those implemented on the target platform, combining gates where possible to optimize the circuit.

Using the barrier() method.   The barrier() method takes as an optional argument the qubit wires on which to place a barrier. If no argument is supplied, a barrier is placed across all of the quantum wires. This method creates a Barrier instance (see "Barrier" on page 151).

The following code snippet demonstrates using the barrier() method with and without arguments:

```
qc = QuantumCircuit(2)
qc.h([0,1])
```

```
qc.barrier()
qc.x(0)
qc.x(0)
qc.s(1)
qc.barrier([1])
qc.s(1)
qc.draw()
```

Figure 1-4 shows the resultant circuit.

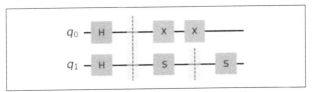

Figure 1-4. Example circuit using the barrier() method

Notice that the S gates in the circuit are separated by a barrier and therefore are not candidates to be combined into a Z gate. However, the X gates may be combined by removing both of them, as they cancel one another out.

Measuring a quantum circuit

The methods commonly used to measure quantum circuits are measure() and measure_all(). The former is useful when the quantum circuit contains classical wires on which to receive the result of a measurement. The latter is useful when the quantum circuit doesn't have any classical wires. These methods create Measure instances (see "Measure" on page 152).

Using the measure() method. The measure() method takes two arguments:

- The qubit wires to be measured
- The classical wires on which to store the resulting bits

This code snippet uses the measure() method, and Figure 1-5 shows a drawing of the resultant circuit:

```
qc = QuantumCircuit(3, 3)
qc.h([0,1,2])
qc.measure([0,1,2], [0,1,2])
qc.draw()
```

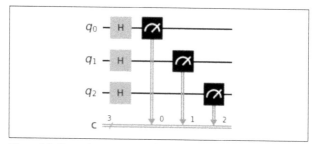

Figure 1-5. Example circuit using the measure() method

Notice that the measure() method appended the requested measurement operations to the circuit.

Using the measure_all() method.   The measure_all() method may be called with no arguments. This code snippet uses the measure_all() method, and Figure 1-6 shows a drawing of the resultant circuit:

```
qc = QuantumCircuit(3)
qc.h([0,1,2])
qc.measure_all()
qc.draw()
```

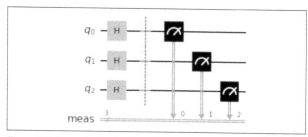

Figure 1-6. Example circuit using the measure_all() method

Notice that the `measure_all()` method created three classical wires and added a barrier to the circuit before appending the measurement operations.

Obtaining information about a quantum circuit

Methods commonly used to obtain information about a quantum circuit include `depth()`, `size()`, and `width()`. These are listed in Table 1-3. Note that the variable qc refers to an instance of QuantumCircuit.

Table 1-3. Methods commonly used to obtain information about a quantum circuit

Names	Example	Notes
depth	qc.depth()	Returns the depth (critical path) of a circuit if directives such as barrier were removed
size	qc.size()	Returns the total number of gate operations in a circuit
width	qc.width()	Returns the sum of qubits wires and classical wires in a circuit

Attributes commonly used to obtain information about a quantum circuit include `clbits`, `data`, `global_phase`, `num_clbits`, `num_qubits`, and `qubits`. These are listed in Table 1-4. Note that variable qc refers to an instance of QuantumCircuit.

Table 1-4. Attributes commonly used to obtain information about a quantum circuit

Names	Example	Notes
clbits	qc.clbits	Obtains the list of classical bits in the order that the registers were added
data	qc.data	Obtains a list of the operations (e.g., gates, barriers, and measurement operations) in the circuit

Names	Example	Notes
global_phase	qc.global_phase	Obtains the global phase of the circuit in radians
num_clbits	qc.num_clbits	Obtains the number of classical wires in the circuit
num_qubits	qc.num_qubits	Obtains the number of quantum wires in the circuit
qubits	qc.qubits	Obtains the list of quantum bits in the order that the registers were added

Manipulating a quantum circuit

Methods commonly used to manipulate quantum circuits include append(), bind_parameters(), compose(), copy(), decompose(), from_qasm_file(), from_qasm_str(), initialize(), reset(), qasm(), to_gate(), and to_instruction().

Using the append() method.   The append() method appends an instruction or gate to the end of the circuit on specified wires, modifying the circuit in place. The following code snippet uses the append() method, and Figure 1-7 shows a drawing of the resultant circuit:

```
from qiskit.circuit.library import CXGate

qc = QuantumCircuit(2)
qc.h(1)
cx_gate = CXGate()
qc.append(cx_gate, [1,0])
qc.draw()
```

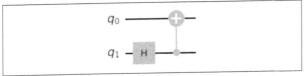

Figure 1-7. Example circuit resulting from the append() method

---

NOTE

The CXGate class (see "CXGate" on page 161) used here is one of the gates defined in the qiskit.circuit.library package. We advise you add the appropriate import statements to code snippets in this book.

Using the bind_parameters() method. The bind_parameters() method binds parameters (see "Creating a Parameter Instance" on page 32) to a quantum circuit. The following code snippet creates a circuit in which there are three parameterized phase gates. Note that the arguments to the Parameter constructors in this code snippet are strings, in this case ones that contain theta characters. Figure 1-8 shows a drawing of the circuit:

```
from qiskit.circuit import QuantumCircuit,\
                           Parameter

theta1 = Parameter('θ1')
theta2 = Parameter('θ2')
theta3 = Parameter('θ3')

qc = QuantumCircuit(3)
qc.h([0,1,2])
qc.p(theta1,0)
qc.p(theta2,1)
qc.p(theta3,2)

qc.draw()
```

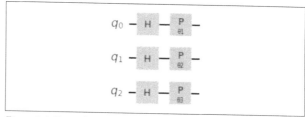

Figure 1-8. Example parameterized circuit

To bind the parameter values to a new circuit, we'll pass a dictionary that contains the parameter references and desired values to the bind_parameters() method. The following code snippet uses this technique, and Figure 1-9 shows the bound circuit in which the phase gate parameters are replaced with the supplied values:

```
b_qc = qc.bind_parameters({theta1: math.pi/8,
                           theta2: math.pi/4,
                           theta3: math.pi/2})

b_qc.draw()
```

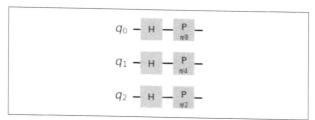

Figure 1-9. Example of bound circuit with the supplied phase gate rotation values

Using the compose() method. The compose() method returns a new circuit composed of the original and another circuit. The following code snippet uses the compose() method, and Figure 1-10 shows a drawing of the resultant circuit:

```
qc = QuantumCircuit(2,2)
qc.h(0)
another_qc = QuantumCircuit(2,2)
another_qc.cx(0,1)
bell_qc = qc.compose(another_qc)
bell_qc.draw()
```

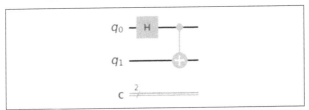

Figure 1-10. Example circuit resulting from the compose() method

Note that a circuit passed into the compose() method is allowed to have fewer quantum or classical wires than the original circuit.

Using the copy() method. The copy() method returns a copy of the original circuit. The following code snippet uses the copy() method:

```
qc = QuantumCircuit(3)
qc.h([0,1,2])
new_qc = qc.copy()
```

Using the decompose() method. The decompose() method returns a new circuit after decomposing the original circuit one level. The following code snippet uses the decompose() method. Figure 1-11 shows a drawing of the resultant circuit in which S, H, and X gates are decomposed into the more fundamental U gate operations (see "UGate" on page 156):

```
qc = QuantumCircuit(2)
qc.h(0)
qc.s(0)
qc.x(1)
```

```
decomposed_qc = qc.decompose()
decomposed_qc.draw()
```

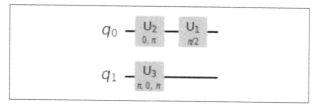

Figure 1-11. Example circuit resulting from the decompose() *method*

Using the from_qasm_file() method. The from_qasm_file()
method returns a new circuit from a file that contains a quantum assembly-language (OpenQASM) program. The following
code snippet uses the from_qasm_file() method:

```
new_qc = QuantumCircuit.from_qasm_file("file.qasm")
```

Using the from_qasm_str() method. The from_qasm_str()
method returns a new circuit from a string that contains an
OpenQASM program. The following code snippet uses the
from_qasm_str() method, and Figure 1-12 shows a drawing of
the resultant circuit:

```
qasm_str = """
OPENQASM 2.0;
include "qelib1.inc";
qreg q[2];
creg c[2];
h q[0];
cx q[0],q[1];
measure q[0] -> c[0];
measure q[1] -> c[1];
"""
new_qc = QuantumCircuit.from_qasm_str(qasm_str)
new_qc.draw()
```

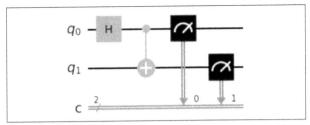

Figure 1-12. Example circuit resulting from the `from_qasm_str()` *method*

Using the initialize() method. The `initialize()` method initializes qubits of a quantum circuit to a given state and is not a unitary operation. The following code uses the `initialize()` method, and Figure 1-13 shows a drawing of the resultant circuit. In this code snippet, the circuit is initialized to the normalized statevector $|11\rangle$:

```
qc = QuantumCircuit(2)
qc.initialize([0, 0, 0, 1])
qc.draw()
```

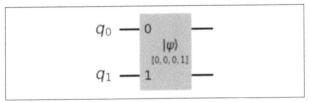

Figure 1-13. Example circuit resulting from the `initialize()` *method*

Using the reset() method. The `reset()` method resets a qubit in a quantum circuit to the $|0\rangle$ state and is not a unitary operation. The following code snippet uses the `reset()` method, and Figure 1-14 shows a drawing of the resultant circuit. Note that the qubit state is $|1\rangle$ before the reset operation. This method creates a `Reset` instance (see "Reset" on page 152):

```
qc = QuantumCircuit(1)
qc.x(0)
qc.reset(0)
qc.draw()
```

Figure 1-14. Example circuit resulting from using the reset() method

Using the qasm() method. The qasm() method returns an Open-
QASM program that represents the quantum circuit. The following code snippet uses the qasm() method, and Example 1-1
shows the resultant OpenQASM program:

```
qc = QuantumCircuit(2, 2)
qc.h(0)
qc.cx(0, 1)
qasm_str = qc.qasm()
print(qasm_str)
```

*Example 1-1. OpenQASM program resulting from the using the
qasm() method*

```
OPENQASM 2.0;
include "qelib1.inc";
qreg q[2];
creg c[2];
h q[0];
cx q[0],q[1];
```

Using the to_gate() method. The to_gate() method creates a
custom *gate* (see "The Gate Class" on page 27) from a quantum
circuit. The following code snippet creates a circuit that will be
converted to a gate, and Figure 1-15 shows a drawing of the
circuit:

```
anti_cnot_qc = QuantumCircuit(2)
anti_cnot_qc.x(0)
```

```
anti_cnot_qc.cx(0,1)
anti_cnot_qc.x(0)

anti_cnot_qc.draw()
```

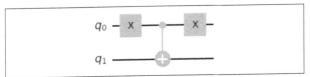

Figure 1-15. Example circuit that will be converted to a gate

This custom gate will implement an anticontrol NOT gate in which the X gate is applied only when the control qubit is |0⟩. The following code snippet creates a circuit that uses this custom gate, and Figure 1-16 shows a decomposed drawing of this circuit:

```
anti_cnot_gate = anti_cnot_qc.to_gate()

qc = QuantumCircuit(3)
qc.x([0,1,2])
qc.append(anti_cnot_gate, [0,2])

qc.decompose().draw()
```

NOTE

A *gate* represents a unitary operation. To create a custom operation that isn't unitary, use the to_instruction() method shown in "Using the to_instruction() method".

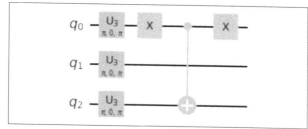

Figure 1-16. Decomposed circuit that uses a gate created by the
to_gate() method

Using the to_instruction() method. The to_instruction()
method creates a custom *instruction* (see "The Instruction
Class" on page 26) from a quantum circuit. The following code
snippet creates a circuit that will be converted to an instruction,
and Figure 1-17 shows a drawing of the circuit:

```
reset_one_qc = QuantumCircuit(1)
reset_one_qc.reset(0)
reset_one_qc.x(0)

reset_one_qc.draw()
```

Figure 1-17. Example circuit that will be converted to an instruction

---

NOTE

An *instruction* represents an operation that isn't necessarily unitary. To create a custom operation that is unitary,
use the to_gate() method shown in "Using the to_gate()
method" on page 20.

This custom instruction will reset a qubit and apply an X gate, in effect resetting the qubit to state $|1\rangle$. The following code snippet creates a circuit that uses this custom instruction, and Figure 1-18 shows a decomposed drawing of this circuit:

```
reset_one_inst = reset_one_qc.to_instruction()

qc = QuantumCircuit(2)
qc.h([0,1])
qc.reset(0)
qc.append(reset_one_inst, [1])

qc.decompose().draw()
```

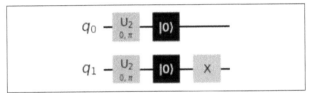

Figure 1-18. Circuit that uses an instruction created by the to_instruction() method

Saving state when running a circuit on AerSimulator

When running a circuit on an AerSimulator backend (see "Using the Aer Simulators" on page 41), the simulator state may be saved in the circuit instance by using the QuantumCircuit methods in Table 1-5. Please note that these methods are available after obtaining an AerSimulator backend.

Table 1-5. Methods used to save simulator state in a circuit instance

Method name	Description
save_state	Saves the simulator state as appropriate for the simulation method
save_density_matrix	Saves the simulator state as a density matrix
save_matrix_product_state	Saves the simulator state as a matrix product state tensor

Method name	Description
save_stabilizer	Saves the simulator state as a Clifford stabilizer
save_statevector	Saves the simulator state as a statevector
save_superop	Saves the simulator state as a superoperator matrix of the run circuit
save_unitary	Saves the simulator state as a unitary matrix of the run circuit

Using the QuantumRegister Class

It is sometimes useful to treat groups of quantum or classical wires as a unit. For example, the control qubits of the CNOT gates in the quantum circuit expressed in the following code snippet, as well as in Figure 1-19, expect three qubits in equal superpositions. The additional quantum wire in the circuit is used as a scratch area whose output is disregarded:

```
from qiskit import QuantumRegister, \
                   ClassicalRegister

qr = QuantumRegister(3, 'q')
scratch = QuantumRegister(1, 'scratch')
cr = ClassicalRegister(3, 'c')
qc = QuantumCircuit(qr, scratch, cr)

qc.h(qr)
qc.x(scratch)
qc.h(scratch)
qc.cx(qr[0], scratch)
qc.cx(qr[2], scratch)
qc.barrier(qr)
qc.h(qr)
qc.measure(qr, cr)

qc.draw()
```

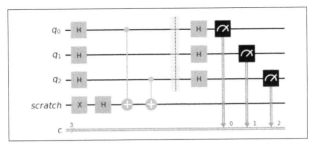

Figure 1-19. Example circuit using the QuantumRegister and ClassicalRegister classes

By defining a QuantumRegister consisting of three qubits, methods such as h(), barrier(), and measure() may be applied to all three wires by passing a QuantumRegister reference. Similarly, defining a ClassicalRegister (see "Using the Classical-Register Class") consisting of three bits enables the measure() method to specify all three classical wires by passing a ClassicalRegister reference. Additionally, the names supplied to the QuantumRegister and ClassicalRegister constructors are displayed on the circuit drawing.

Using QuantumRegister Attributes

Commonly used QuantumRegister attributes include name and size. These are listed in Table 1-6. Note that the variable qr refers to an instance of QuantumRegister.

Table 1-6. Some QuantumRegister attributes

Names	Example	Notes
name	qr.name	Obtains the name of the quantum register
size	qr.size	Obtains the number of qubit wires in the quantum register

Using the ClassicalRegister Class

Please refer to "Using the QuantumRegister Class" on page 24 for reasons to use the ClassicalRegister class.

Using ClassicalRegister Attributes

Commonly used ClassicalRegister attributes include name and size. These are listed in Table 1-7. Note that the variable cr refers to an instance of ClassicalRegister.

Table 1-7. Some ClassicalRegister attributes

Names	Example	Notes
name	cr.name	Obtains the name of the classical register
size	cr.size	Obtains the number of bit wires in the classical register

Instructions and Gates

In Qiskit, all operations that may be applied to a quantum circuit are derived from the Instruction class. Unitary operations are derived from the Gate class, which is a subclass of Instruction. Controlled-unitary operations are derived from the ControlledGate class, which is a subclass of Gate. These classes may be used to define new instructions, unitary gates, and controlled-unitary gates, respectively.

The Instruction Class

The nonunitary operations in Qiskit (such as Measure and Reset) are direct subclasses of Instruction. Although it is possible to define your own custom instructions by subclassing Instruction, another way is to use the to_instruction() method of the QuantumCircuit class (see an example of this in "Using the to_instruction() method" on page 22).

Methods in the Instruction class include copy(), repeat(), and reverse_ops(). These are listed in Table 1-8. Note that the variable inst refers to an instance of Instruction.

Table 1-8. Commonly used methods in the Instruction class

Names	Example	Notes
copy	inst.copy("My inst")	Returns a copy of the instruction, giving the supplied name to the copy
repeat	inst.repeat(2)	Returns an instruction with this instruction repeated a given number of times
reverse_ops	inst.reverse_ops()	Returns an instruction with its operations in reverse order

Commonly used attributes in the Instruction class include definition and params. These are listed in Table 1-9. Note that the variable inst refers to an instance of Instruction.

Table 1-9. Commonly used attributes in the Instruction class

Names	Example	Notes
definition	inst.definition	Returns the definition in terms of basic gates
params	inst.params	Obtains the parameters to the instruction

The Gate Class

The unitary operations in Qiskit (such as HGate and XGate) are subclasses of Gate. Although it is possible to define your own custom gates by subclassing Gate, another way is to use the to_gate() method of the QuantumCircuit class (see an example of this in "Using the to_gate() method" on page 20).

Commonly used methods in the Gate class include the Instruction methods listed in Table 1-8 as well as control(), inverse(), power(), and to_matrix(). These are all listed in Table 1-10. Note that the variable gate refers to an instance of Gate.

Table 1-10. Commonly used methods in the Gate class

Names	Example	Notes
control	gate.control(1)	Given a number of control qubits, returns a controlled version of the gate
copy	gate.copy("My gate")	Returns a copy of the gate, giving the supplied name to the copy
inverse	gate.inverse()	Returns the inverse of the gate
power	gate.power(2)	Returns the gate raised to a given floating-point power
repeat	gate.repeat(3)	Returns a gate with this gate repeated a given number of times
reverse_ops	gate.reverse_ops()	Returns a gate with its operations in reverse order
to_matrix	gate.to_matrix()	Returns an array for the gate's unitary matrix

Commonly used attributes in the Gate class include the Instruction attributes listed in Table 1-9 as well as label. These are all listed in Table 1-11. Note that the variable gate refers to an instance of Gate.

Table 1-11. Commonly used attributes in the Gate class

Names	Example	Notes
definition	gate.definition	Returns the definition in terms of basic gates
label	gate.label	Obtains the label for the instruction
params	gate.params	Obtains the parameters to the instruction

The ControlledGate Class

The controlled-unitary operations in Qiskit (such as CZGate and CCXGate) are subclasses of ControlledGate, which is a subclass of Gate.

Commonly used methods in the ControlledGate class are the Gate methods listed in Table 1-10

Commonly used attributes in the ControlledGate class include the Gate attributes listed in Table 1-11 as well as num_ctrl_qubits and ctrl_state.

Using the num_ctrl_qubits attribute

The num_ctrl_qubits attribute holds an integer that represents the number of control qubits in a ControlledGate. The following code snippet, whose printed output would be 2, uses the num_ctrl_qubits attribute of a Toffoli gate:

```
from qiskit.circuit.library import CCXGate

toffoli = CCXGate()
print(toffoli.num_ctrl_qubits)
```

Using the ctrl_state() method

A ControlledGate may have one or more control qubits, each of which may actually be either control or *anticontrol* qubits (see the anticontrol example in "Using the to_gate() method" on page 20). The ctrl_state attribute holds an integer whose binary value represents which qubits are control qubits and which are anticontrol qubits. Specifically, the binary digit 1 represents a control qubit, and the binary digit 0 represents an anticontrol qubit.

The ctrl_state attribute supports both accessing and modifying its value. The following code snippet uses the ctrl_state attribute in which the binary value 10 causes the topmost control qubit to be an anticontrol qubit. Figure 1-20 shows a drawing of the resultant circuit:

```
toffoli = CCXGate()
toffoli.ctrl_state = 2

toffoli.definition.draw()
```

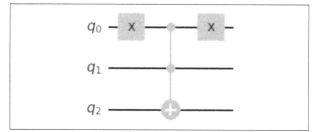

Figure 1-20. Toffoli gate with a control qubit and an anticontrol qubit

Defining a custom controlled gate

Although it is possible to define your own custom controlled gates by subclassing ControlledGate, another way is to follow these two steps:

1. Create a custom gate with the to_gate() method of the QuantumCircuit class (see an example of this in "Using the to_gate() method" on page 20).

2. Add control qubits to your custom gate by using the control() method shown in Table 1-10.

We'll follow those two steps to define a custom controlled gate that applies a $\pi/16$ phase rotation when both of its control qubits are $|1\rangle$. First, the following code snippet defines a circuit that contains a $\pi/16$ P gate and converts it to a custom gate, with Figure 1-21 showing a drawing of the custom gate:

```
from qiskit import QuantumCircuit
import math

p16_qc = QuantumCircuit(1)
p16_qc.p(math.pi/16, 0)
```

```
p16_gate = p16_qc.to_gate()

p16_gate.definition.draw()
```

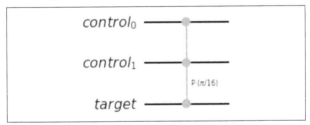

Figure 1-21. Custom π/16 phase gate drawing

Second, the following code snippet uses the control() method to create a ControlledGate from our custom gate, and Figure 1-22 shows a drawing of the custom controlled gate:

```
ctrl_p16 = p16_gate.control(2)

ctrl_p16.definition.draw()
```

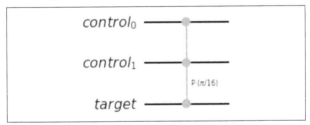

Figure 1-22. Custom controlled π/16 phase gate drawing

We'll leverage the append() method (see "Using the append() method" on page 14) in the following code snippet to use our custom controlled gate in a quantum circuit. Figure 1-23 shows a drawing of the circuit:

```
qc = QuantumCircuit(4)
qc.h([0,1,2,3])
qc.append(ctrl_p16,[0,1,3])

qc.decompose().draw()
```

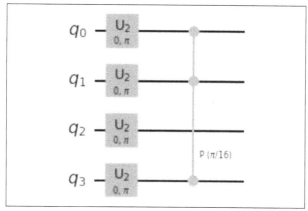

Figure 1-23. Decomposed circuit that uses the custom controlled gate

Parameterized Quantum Circuits

It is sometimes useful to create a quantum circuit in which values may be supplied at runtime. This capability is available in Qiskit using *parameterized circuits*, implemented in part by the Parameter and ParameterVector classes.

Creating a Parameter Instance

The Parameter class is used to represent a parameter in a quantum circuit. See "Using the bind_parameters() method" on page 15 for an example of defining and using a parameterized circuit. As shown in that example, a parameter may be created by supplying a unicode string to its constructor as follows:

```
theta1 = Parameter("θ1")
```

The Parameter object reference named theta1 may subsequently be used in the bind_parameters() or alternatively the assign_parameters() method of the QuantumCircuit class.

Using the ParameterVector Class

The `ParameterVector` class may be leveraged to create and use parameters as a collection instead of individual variables. The following code snippet creates a circuit in which there are three parameterized phase gates. Figure 1-24 shows a drawing of the circuit:

```
from qiskit.circuit import QuantumCircuit,\
                            ParameterVector

theta = ParameterVector('θ', 3)

qc = QuantumCircuit(3)
qc.h([0,1,2])
qc.p(theta[0],0)
qc.p(theta[1],1)
qc.p(theta[2],2)

qc.draw()
```

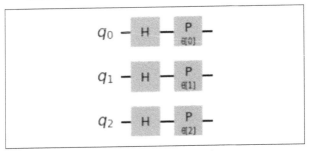

Figure 1-24. Example of a parameterized circuit leveraging `ParameterVector`

To bind the parameter values to a new circuit, we'll pass a dictionary that contains the `ParameterVector` reference and desired list of values to the `bind_parameters()` method.

The following code snippet shows this technique, and Figure 1-25 shows the bound circuit in which the phase gate parameters are replaced with the supplied values:

```
import math

b_qc = qc.bind_parameters({theta: [math.pi/8,
                                   math.pi/4,
                                   math.pi/2]})

b_qc.draw()
```

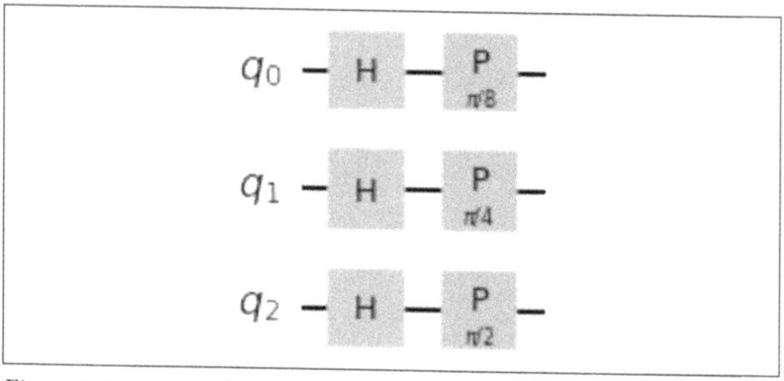

Figure 1-25. Example of bound circuit with the supplied phase gate rotation values

## CHAPTER 2

Running Quantum Circuits

Qiskit supports running quantum circuits on a wide variety of quantum simulators and devices. We'll explore relevant classes and functions, most of which are located in the following modules:

`qiskit.providers.basicaer`

> This module contains a basic set of simulators implemented in Python, which are often referred to as *BasicAer* simulators.

`qiskit.providers.aer`

> This module contains a comprehensive set of high-performance simulators, which are often referred to as *Aer* simulators.

`qiskit.providers`

> This module contains classes that support these simulators as well as provide access to real quantum devices.

Regardless of the quantum simulator or device on which you choose to run a circuit, you may follow these steps:

1. Identify the appropriate *provider* (either `BasicAer`, `Aer`, or a quantum device provider). A provider's purpose is to

get *backend* objects that enable executing circuits on a quantum simulator or device.

2. Obtain a reference to the desired *backend* from the provider. A backend provides the interface between Qiskit and the hardware or simulator that will execute circuits.

3. Using the backend, run the circuit on the simulator or device. This returns an object that represents the *job* in which the circuit is being run.

4. Interact with the job for purposes such as checking status and getting its *result* after completing.

Using the BasicAer Simulators

As with any backend provider, a list of available BasicAer backends may be obtained by calling the provider's backends() method as shown in the following code snippet:

```
from qiskit import BasicAer

print(BasicAer.backends())


output:
[<QasmSimulatorPy('qasm_simulator')>,
 <StatevectorSimulatorPy('statevector_simulator')>,
 <UnitarySimulatorPy('unitary_simulator')>]
```

Notice that the output shows a Python list containing three BasicAer backends, each of which represents a simulator implemented by a corresponding class. A reference to the desired backend may be obtained by calling the provider's get_backend() method as shown in the following subsection.

Using the BasicAer qasm_simulator Backend

Notice that the desired backend in this example is the qasm_simulator, whose main purpose is to run a circuit and hold its measurement outcomes:

```
from qiskit import QuantumCircuit, BasicAer, \
                                   transpile

qc = QuantumCircuit(2)
qc.h(0)
qc.cx(0, 1)
qc.measure_all()  ❶

backend = BasicAer.get_backend("qasm_simulator")  ❷
tqc = transpile(qc, backend)  ❸
job = backend.run(tqc, shots=1000)  ❹
result = job.result()  ❺
counts = result.get_counts(tqc)  ❻
print(counts)


output:  ❼
  {'00': 495, '11': 505}
```

Let's take a closer look at some relevant lines in the code snippet:

❶ The BasicAer qasm_simulator backend is useful for circuits that contain measurement instructions.

❷ A reference to the qasm_simulator backend (implemented by the QasmSimulatorPy class) is obtained.

❸ The circuit is transpiled with the transpile() function to use only gates available on the BasicAer qasm_simulator.

❹ The transpiled circuit and number of shots to perform is passed to the run() method of the BasicAer qasm_simula tor backend. The run() method returns a BasicAerJob instance.

❺ The result of running the circuit (held in a qiskit.Result instance) is obtained with the result() method of the BasicAerJob instance.

❻ A Python dictionary containing the measurement outcomes per basis state is obtained with the get_counts() method of the Result instance.

❼ The measurement outcomes are printed in the output.

Using the BasicAer statevector_simulator Backend

The following code snippet uses the statevector_simulator, whose main purpose is to run a circuit and hold its resultant statevector:

```
from qiskit import QuantumCircuit, BasicAer, \
                                    transpile

qc = QuantumCircuit(2) ❶
qc.h(0)
qc.cx(0, 1)

backend = \
    BasicAer.get_backend("statevector_simulator") ❷
tqc = transpile(qc, backend) ❸
job = backend.run(tqc) ❹
result = job.result() ❺
statevector = result.get_statevector(tqc, 4) ❻
print(statevector)


output: ❼
  [0.7071+0.j 0.+0.j 0.+0.j 0.7071+0.j]
```

Let's take a closer look at some relevant lines in the code snippet:

❶ Because measurement instructions collapse quantum states, the BasicAer statevector_simulator backend is most useful for circuits without measurement instructions. The statevector_simulator is "one-shot," so if there are measurements, you could get a different statevector each time.

❷ A reference to the statevector_simulator backend (implemented by the StatevectorSimulatorPy class) is obtained.

❸ The circuit is transpiled with the transpile() function to use only gates available on the BasicAer statevector_ simulator.

❹ The transpiled circuit is passed to the run() method of the BasicAer statevector_simulator backend. The run() method returns a BasicAerJob instance.

❺ The result of running the circuit (held in a qiskit.Result instance) is obtained with the result() method of the BasicAerJob instance.

❻ A list of complex probability amplitudes containing up to four decimal places that express a statevector is obtained with the get_statevector() method of the Result instance.

❼ The statevector is printed in the output.

Using the BasicAer unitary_simulator Backend

To complete our tour of BasicAer backends, we'll take a look at the unitary_simulator in the following code snippet, whose main purpose is to run a circuit and hold a unitary matrix that represents the circuit:

```
from qiskit import QuantumCircuit, BasicAer, \
                                    transpile

qc = QuantumCircuit(2) ❶
qc.h(0)
qc.cx(0, 1)

backend = \
    BasicAer.get_backend("unitary_simulator") ❷
tqc = transpile(qc, backend) ❸
```

```
job = backend.run(tqc) ❹
result = job.result() ❺
unitary = result.get_unitary(tqc, 4) ❻
print(unitary)


output: ❼
  [[ 0.7071+0.0000j  0.7071-0.0000j
     0.0000+0.0000j  0.0000+0.0000j]]
   [ 0.0000+0.0000j  0.0000+0.0000j
     0.7071+0.0000j -0.7071+0.0000j]]
   [ 0.0000+0.0000j  0.0000+0.0000j
     0.7071+0.0000j  0.7071-0.0000j]]
   [ 0.7071+0.0000j -0.7071+0.0000j
     0.0000+0.0000j  0.0000+0.0000j]]]
```

Let's take a closer look at some relevant lines in the code
snippet:

❶ The BasicAer unitary_simulator backend is useful only
    for circuits without measurement or reset instructions, as
    they are not supported by the unitary_simulator.

❷ A reference to the unitary_simulator backend (imple-
    mented by the UnitarySimulatorPy class) is obtained.

❸ The circuit is transpiled with the transpile() function to
    use only gates that are available on the BasicAer unitary_
    simulator.

❹ The transpiled circuit is passed to the run() method of the
    BasicAer unitary_simulator backend. The run() method
    returns a BasicAerJob instance.

❺ The result of running the circuit (held in a qiskit.Result
    instance) is obtained with the result() method of the
    BasicAerJob instance.

❻ A square matrix of complex numbers that express the circuit's unitary matrix (transition amplitudes) is obtained with the get_unitary() method of the Result instance.

❼ The unitary matrix is printed in the output.

NOTE

As an alternative to calling the run() method of any of the simulator backends, you could call the execute() function. This function is located in the qiskit.execute_function module, and it relieves you of the responsibility of calling the transpile() function.

Now we'll turn our attention to the qiskit.providers.aer module, which contains a comprehensive set of high-performance simulators often referred to as *Aer* simulators.

Using the Aer Simulators

As with any backend provider, a list of available Aer backends may be obtained by calling the provider's backends() method as shown in the following code snippet:

```
from qiskit import Aer

print(Aer.backends())


output:
[AerSimulator('aer_simulator'),
AerSimulator('aer_simulator_statevector'),
AerSimulator('aer_simulator_density_matrix'),
AerSimulator('aer_simulator_stabilizer'),
AerSimulator('aer_simulator_matrix_product_state'),
AerSimulator('aer_simulator_extended_stabilizer'),
AerSimulator('aer_simulator_unitary'),
AerSimulator('aer_simulator_superop'),
```

```
        QasmSimulator('qasm_simulator'),
        StatevectorSimulator('statevector_simulator'),
        UnitarySimulator('unitary_simulator'),
        PulseSimulator('pulse_simulator')]
```

We'll examine several of these `Aer` simulator backends, beginning with the three legacy simulators that resemble their
`BasicAer` counterparts. These legacy simulators are faster than
the Python-implemented `BasicAer` simulators but have similar
APIs.

Using the Aer Legacy Simulators

The `Aer` provider has received greatly enhanced functionality
with the introduction of the `AerSimulator` and `PulseSimulator`
classes. In addition, three of the `Aer` legacy simulator backends remain. These backends are `qasm_simulator`, `statevec
tor_simulator`, and `unitary_simulator`.

The code for using these `Aer` legacy simulators is nearly identical to the code for using their `BasicAer` counterparts. The
only difference is that instead of using the `BasicAer` provider,
you'd use the `Aer` provider. To try this out, run each of the
code snippets in "Using the BasicAer Simulators" on page 36,
substituting `BasicAer` with `Aer`.

Let's move on to the main simulator backend of the `Aer` provider, named `AerSimulator`.

Using the AerSimulator Backend

The `AerSimulator` backend is very versatile, offering many
types of simulation methods, the default being `automatic`. The
`automatic` simulation method allows the simulation method to
be selected automatically based on the circuit and noise model.

Using the AerSimulator to hold measurement results

In the following code snippet, the simulator will hold measurement results due to the presence of measurement instructions
in the circuit:

```
from qiskit import QuantumCircuit,Aer,transpile

qc = QuantumCircuit(2)
qc.h(0)
qc.cx(0, 1)
qc.measure_all()  ❶

backend = Aer.get_backend("aer_simulator")  ❷
tqc = transpile(qc, backend)  ❸
job = backend.run(tqc, shots=1000)  ❹
result = job.result()  ❺
counts = result.get_counts(tqc)  ❻
print(counts)


output:  ❼
  {'00': 516, '11': 484}
```

Let's take a closer look at some relevant lines in the code snippet:

❶ The AerSimulator with automatic simulation method will hold measurement results when measurement instructions are present.

❷ A reference to an AerSimulator backend with the auto matic simulation method is obtained by passing "aer_ simulator" into the get_backend() method.

❸ The circuit is transpiled with the transpile() function to use only gates available on this backend.

❹ The transpiled circuit and number of shots to perform is passed to the run() method of the backend. The run() method returns an AerJob instance.

❺ The result of running the circuit (held in a qiskit.Result instance) is obtained with the result() method of the AerJob instance.

❻ A Python dictionary containing the measurement outcomes per basis state is obtained with the get_counts()
method of the Result instance.

❼ The measurement outcomes are printed in the output.

Next we'll use the AerSimulator as a statevector simulator.

Using the AerSimulator to calculate and hold a statevector

In the following code snippet, the simulator will calculate and
hold a statevector:

```python
from qiskit import QuantumCircuit,Aer,transpile

qc = QuantumCircuit(2) ❶
qc.h(0)
qc.cx(0, 1)

backend = Aer.get_backend("aer_simulator") ❷
qc.save_statevector() ❸

tqc = transpile(qc, backend) ❹
job = backend.run(tqc) ❺
result = job.result() ❻
statevector = result.get_statevector(tqc, 4) ❼
print(statevector)


output: ❽
  [0.7071+0.j 0.+0.j 0.+0.j 0.7071+0.j]
```

Let's take a closer look at some relevant lines in the code
snippet:

❶ Because measurement instructions collapse quantum
states, AerSimulator statevector simulator functionality is
most useful for circuits that do not have measurement
instructions.

❷ A reference to an `AerSimulator` backend with the auto matic simulation method is obtained by passing "aer_ simulator" into the `get_backend()` method.

❸ The `save_statevector()` method saves the current simulator quantum state as a statevector. See "Saving state when running a circuit on AerSimulator" on page 23 for other methods that save simulator state in a quantum circuit.

❹ The circuit is transpiled with the `transpile()` function to use only gates available on this backend.

❺ The transpiled circuit is passed to the `run()` method of the backend. The `run()` method returns an `AerJob` instance.

❻ The result of running the circuit (held in a `qiskit.Result` instance) is obtained with the `result()` method of the `AerJob` instance.

❼ A list of complex probability amplitudes that express the saved statevector is obtained with the `get_statevector()` method of the `Result` instance.

❽ The statevector is printed in the output.

Now we'll use the `AerSimulator` as a unitary simulator.

Using the AerSimulator to calculate and hold a unitary

In the following code snippet, the simulator will calculate and hold a circuit's unitary:

```
from qiskit import QuantumCircuit,Aer,transpile

qc = QuantumCircuit(2) ❶
qc.h(0)
qc.cx(0, 1)

backend = Aer.get_backend("aer_simulator") ❷
qc.save_unitary() ❸
```

```
tqc = transpile(qc, backend)  ❹
job = backend.run(tqc)  ❺
result = job.result()  ❻
unitary = result.get_unitary(qc, 4)  ❼
print(unitary)


output:  ❽
  [[ 0.7071+0.0000j  0.7071-0.0000j
     0.0000+0.0000j  0.0000+0.0000j]
   [ 0.0000+0.0000j  0.0000+0.0000j
     0.7071+0.0000j -0.7071+0.0000j]
   [ 0.0000+0.0000j  0.0000+0.0000j
     0.7071+0.0000j  0.7071-0.0000j]
   [ 0.7071+0.0000j -0.7071+0.0000j
     0.0000+0.0000j  0.0000+0.0000j]]
```

Let's take a closer look at some relevant lines in the code snippet:

❶ AerSimulator unitary simulator functionality is only useful for circuits without measurement or reset instructions.

❷ A reference to an AerSimulator backend with the auto matic simulation method is obtained by passing "aer_ simulator" into the get_backend() method.

❸ The save_unitary() method saves the circuit's unitary matrix. See "Saving state when running a circuit on AerSimulator" on page 23 for other methods that save simulator state in a quantum circuit.

❹ The circuit is transpiled with the transpile() function to use only gates available on this backend.

❺ The transpiled circuit is passed to the run() method of the backend. The run() method returns an AerJob instance.

❻ The result of running the circuit (held in a `qiskit.Result` instance) is obtained with the `result()` method of the `AerJob` instance.

❼ A square matrix of complex numbers that express that the saved unitary matrix is obtained with the `get_unitary()` method of the `Result` instance.

❽ The unitary matrix is printed in the output.

Now we'll discuss using the `AerSimulator` for additional simulation methods.

Using the AerSimulator for additional simulation methods

So far we've examined examples of using the `AerSimulator` backend with the `automatic` simulation method to run a circuit and hold either its measurement results, statevector, or unitary matrix. The `AerSimulator` backend is capable of additional simulation methods, automatically selecting them based on the circuit and noise model. Simulation methods may also be set explicitly.

Using set_options() to update the simulation method. The simulation method for an `AerSimulator` backend may be explicitly updated by calling `set_options()`, passing the desired simulation method from Table 2-1 as a keyword argument. For example, the following code snippet may be used to update an `AerSimulator` backend to use the `density_matrix` simulation method:

```
backend = Aer.get_backend("aer_simulator")
backend.set_options(method="density_matrix")
```

Getting a backend with a preconfigured simulation method. Each of the Aer simulation methods has a corresponding string that may be passed into the `get_backend()` method. These strings are output in the first snippet of this section and may be formed by appending a simulation method from Table 2-1 to "aer_simulator_". For example, the following code snippet may be used to get an AerSimulator backend preconfigured with the density_matrix simulation method:

```
Aer.get_backend("aer_simulator_density_matrix")
```

Passing a simulation method into run(). The simulation method for an AerSimulator backend may be explicitly overridden for a single execution. This is achieved by passing the desired simulation method from Table 2-1 as a keyword argument into the run() method. For example, the following code snippet, in which tqc is a transpiled circuit, may be used to override the simulation method of an AerSimulator backend to use the density_matrix simulation method:

```
backend = Aer.get_backend("aer_simulator")
backend.run(tqc, method="density_matrix")
```

Table 2-1 contains a list of the AerSimulator simulation methods.

Table 2-1. AerSimulator simulation methods

Name	Description
automatic	Default simulation method that selects the simulation method automatically based on the circuit and noise model.
density_ matrix	Density matrix simulation that may sample measurement outcomes from noisy circuits with all measurements at the end of the circuit.
extended_ stabilizer	An approximate simulation for Clifford + T circuits based on a state decomposition into ranked-stabilizer state.
matrix_prod uct_state	A tensor-network statevector simulator that uses a matrix product state (MPS) representation for the state.
stabilizer	An efficient Clifford stabilizer state simulator that can simulate noisy Clifford circuits if all errors in the noise model are also Clifford errors.

Name	Description
statevector	Statevector simulation that can sample measurement outcomes from ideal circuits with all measurements at the end of the circuit. For noisy simulations, each shot samples a randomly sampled noisy circuit from the noise model.
superop	Superoperator matrix simulation of an ideal or noisy circuit. This simulates the superoperator matrix of the circuit itself rather than the evolution of an initial quantum state.
unitary	Unitary matrix simulation of an ideal circuit. This simulates the unitary matrix of the circuit itself rather than the evolution of an initial quantum state.

Notice that some of the simulation method descriptions in Table 2-1 mention simulating noisy circuits. The AerSimulator supports this by allowing a noise model to be supplied that expresses error characteristics of a real or hypothetical quantum device.

Supplying a noise model to an AerSimulator backend

In the following code snippet, a simple custom noise model is created and supplied to an AerSimulator backend:

```
from qiskit import QuantumCircuit, Aer, transpile
from qiskit.providers.aer.noise import \
        NoiseModel, depolarizing_error

err_1 = depolarizing_error(0.95, 1)  ❶
err_2 = depolarizing_error(0.01, 2)
noise_model = NoiseModel()
noise_model.add_all_qubit_quantum_error(err_1,
                            ['u1', 'u2', 'u3'])
noise_model.add_all_qubit_quantum_error(err_2,
                                        ['cx'])

qc = QuantumCircuit(2)
qc.h(0)
qc.cx(0, 1)
qc.measure_all()
```

```
backend = Aer.get_backend("aer_simulator")
backend.set_options(noise_model=noise_model) ❷
tqc = transpile(qc, backend)
job = backend.run(tqc, shots=1000)
result = job.result()
counts = result.get_counts(tqc)
print(counts)

output: ❸
  {'00': 508, '01': 3, '10': 3, '11': 486}
```

Let's take a closer look at some relevant lines in the code snippet:

❶ Build a simple noise model using classes and functions from the `qiskit.providers.aer.noise` module.

❷ Supply the noise model to the `AerSimulator` backend with its `set_options` method.

❸ Measurement outcomes printed in the output reflect the circuit noise.

This example supplied a noise model to an `AerSimulator` backend. In the next section, we'll create an `AerSimulator` backend from the characteristics of a real quantum device.

Creating an AerSimulator backend from a real device

To simulate a real quantum device, mimicking its configuration and noise model, you may use the from_backend() method of the `AerSimulator` class as shown in the following code snippet:

```
from qiskit import QuantumCircuit, transpile
from qiskit.providers.aer import AerSimulator
from qiskit.test.mock import FakeVigo

qc = QuantumCircuit(2)
qc.h(0)
qc.cx(0, 1)
qc.measure_all()
```

```
device_backend = FakeVigo()  ❶
backend = \
    AerSimulator.from_backend(device_backend)  ❷
tqc = transpile(qc, backend)
job = backend.run(tqc, shots=1000)
result = job.result()
counts = result.get_counts(tqc)
print(counts)

output:  ❸
  {'00': 494, '01': 49, '10': 39, '11': 418}
```

Let's take a closer look at some relevant lines in the code snippet:

❶ Because available real hardware devices are continually updating, we're using device configuration and noise data that exists in a Qiskit library for this example. To obtain a device backend from a quantum device provider, you could use the following code snippet, where provider is a reference to the provider, and device is the name of the device:

```
device_backend = provider.get_backend("device")
```

❷ An AerSimulator backend is created using the supplied device backend.

❸ The measurement outcomes are printed in the output.

Monitoring Job Status and Obtaining Results

When running a quantum circuit, a reference to a job (currently a subclass of qiskit.providers.JobV1) is returned. This job reference may be used to monitor its status as well as to obtain a reference to a qiskit.result.Result instance. This Result reference may be used to obtain relevant results data from the experiment. Tables 2-2, 2-3, and 2-4 describe some of the commonly used methods and attributes in these classes.

Table 2-2. Commonly used `qiskit.providers.JobV1` methods

Method name	Description
`job_id`	Returns a unique identifier for this job.
`backend`	Returns a reference to a subclass of `qiskit.providers.BackendV1` used for this job.
`status`	Returns the status of this job, for example, `JobStatus.QUEUED`, `JobStatus.RUNNING`, or `JobStatus.DONE`.
`cancel`	Makes an attempt to cancel the job.
`canceled`	Returns a Boolean that indicates whether the job has been canceled.
`running`	Returns a Boolean that indicates whether the job is actively running on the quantum simulator or device.
`done`	Returns a Boolean that indicates whether the job has successfully run.
`in_final_state`	Returns a Boolean that indicates whether the job has finished. If so, it is in one of the final states: `JobStatus.CANCELED`, `JobStatus.DONE`, or `JobStatus.ERROR`.
`wait_for_final_state`	Polls the job status for a given duration at a given interval, calling an optional callback method. Returns when the job is in one of the final states or the given duration has expired.

Method name	Description
result	Returns an instance of qiskit .result.Result that holds relevant results data from the experiment.

Table 2-3. Commonly used qiskit.result.Result methods

Method name	Description
get_counts	Returns a dictionary containing the count of measurement outcomes per basis state, if available.
get_memory	Returns a list containing a basis state resulting from each shot, if available. Requires that the memory option is True.
get_statevector	Returns a list of complex probability amplitudes that express a saved statevector, if available.
get_unitary	Return a unitary matrix of complex numbers that represents the circuit, if available.
data	Returns the raw data for an experiment.
to_dict	Returns a dictionary representation of the results attribute (see Table 2-4).

Table 2-4. Commonly used qiskit.result.Result attributes

Attribute name	Description
backend_name	Holds the name of the backend quantum simulator or device.
backend_ version	Holds the version of the backend quantum simulator or device.
job_id	Holds a unique identifier for the job that produced this result.
results	List containing results of experiments run. Note that all of our examples run just one circuit at a time.
success	Indicates whether experiments ran successfully.

## CHAPTER 3

Visualizing Quantum Measurements and States

In addition to drawing circuits (see "Drawing a quantum circuit" on page 9), Qiskit provides visualizations for data such as measurement counts and quantum states.

Visualizing Measurement Counts

To visualize experiments that result in measurement counts, Qiskit contains the plot_histogram() function.

Using the plot_histogram Function

The plot_histogram() function takes a dictionary containing measurement counts and plots them in a bar graph with one bar per basis state. We'll demonstrate this function in Example 3-1 by plotting the measurement counts from the example in "Using the AerSimulator to hold measurement results" on page 42.

Example 3-1. Using the plot_histogram() function to plot measurement counts

```
from qiskit import QuantumCircuit,Aer,transpile
from qiskit.visualization import plot_histogram

qc = QuantumCircuit(2)
qc.h(0)
qc.cx(0, 1)
qc.measure_all()

backend = Aer.get_backend("aer_simulator")
tqc = transpile(qc, backend)
job = backend.run(tqc, shots=1000)
result = job.result()
counts = result.get_counts(tqc)

plot_histogram(counts)
```

Figure 3-1 shows the counts expressed as probabilities in a bar graph.

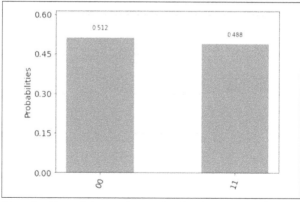

Figure 3-1. Example bar graph using the plot_histogram() function

Table 3-1 contains a list of commonly used `plot_histogram` parameters. This is implemented with `matplotlib`, which uses parameters shown in the table, such as `figsize`.

Table 3-1. Commonly used `plot_histogram` parameters

Parameter name	Description
data	Dictionary, or list of dictionaries, containing measurement counts.
figsize	Tuple containing figure size in inches.
color	String or list of strings for bar colors.
legend	A list of strings to label the data. The number of entries must match the number of dictionaries in the data parameter.
bar_labels	Boolean that causes each bar to be labeled with probability values.
title	A string to label the plot title.

Visualizing Quantum States

Qiskit contains several functions for visualizing statevectors and density matrices, including the following:

- plot_state_qsphere()
- plot_state_city()
- plot_bloch_multivector()
- plot_state_hinton()
- plot_state_paulivec()

Using the plot_state_qsphere Function

The `plot_state_qsphere()` function takes a statevector or density matrix and represents it on a *Q-sphere*. Often confused with a Bloch sphere, the Q-sphere is great for visualizing multi-qubit quantum states. We'll demonstrate this function in

Example 3-2 by plotting the statevector from a circuit containing a *quantum Fourier transform* (QFT).

Example 3-2. Using the `plot_state_qsphere()` function to plot a statevector

```
from qiskit import QuantumCircuit,Aer,transpile
from qiskit.visualization import plot_state_qsphere
from math import pi

backend = \
    Aer.get_backend("aer_simulator_statevector")

qc = QuantumCircuit(3)
qc.rx(pi, 0)
qc.ry(pi/8, 2)
qc.swap(0, 2)
qc.h(0)
qc.cp(pi/2,0, 1)
qc.cp(pi/4, 0, 2)
qc.h(1)
qc.cp(pi/2, 1, 2)
qc.h(2)
qc.save_statevector()

tqc = transpile(qc, backend)
job = backend.run(tqc)
result = job.result()
statevector = result.get_statevector()

plot_state_qsphere(statevector)
```

Figure 3-2 shows a Q-sphere with a point for each basis state. The size of each point is proportional to its measurement probability, and a point's color corresponds to its phase. Notice that the basis states are placed on the poles and latitude lines of the sphere according to their *Hamming weights* (number of ones in their basis states), starting from all zeros at the top and all ones at the bottom.

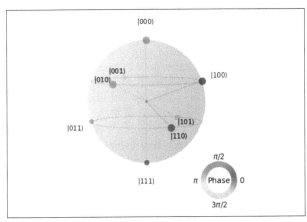

Figure 3-2. Example Q-sphere produced by the
plot_state_qsphere() function

Table 3-2 contains a list of commonly used plot_state_qsphere
parameters.

Table 3-2. Commonly used plot_state_qsphere parameters

Parameter name	Description
state	Statevector, DensityMatrix, or ndarray (a NumPy type) containing complex numbers that represents a pure or mixed quantum state
figsize	Tuple containing figure size in inches
show_state_labels	Boolean indicating whether to show labels for each basis state
show_state_phases	Boolean indicating whether to show the phase for each basis state
use_degrees	Boolean indicating whether to use degrees for the phase values in the plot

Using the plot_state_city Function

The plot_state_city() function takes a statevector or density matrix and represents it on a pair of three-dimensional bar graphs also known as a *cityscape*. We'll demonstrate this function in Example 3-3 by plotting the density matrix from the *mixed state* example in "Using the DensityMatrix Class" on page 91.

Example 3-3. Using the plot_state_city() function to plot a density matrix for a mixed state

```
from qiskit.quantum_info import DensityMatrix, \
                                    Operator
from qiskit.visualization import plot_state_city

dens_mat = 0.5*DensityMatrix.from_label('11') + \
  0.5*DensityMatrix.from_label('+0')
tt_op = Operator.from_label('TT')
dens_mat = dens_mat.evolve(tt_op)

plot_state_city(dens_mat)
```

Figure 3-3 shows a pair of 3D bar graphs that represent the complex numbers in the density matrix. The left 3D bar graph represents the real parts, and the right 3D bar graph represents the imaginary parts. See "Using the DensityMatrix Class" for a discussion on the *mixed state* in this example.

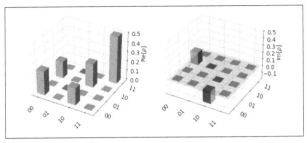

Figure 3-3. 3D bar graphs produced by the `plot_state_city()` function

Table 3-3 lists commonly used `plot_state_city` parameters.

Table 3-3. Commonly used `plot_state_city` parameters

Parameter name	Description
state	Statevector, DensityMatrix, or ndarray (a NumPy type) containing complex numbers that represents a pure or mixed quantum state
title	A string to label the plot title
figsize	Tuple containing figure size in inches
color	List with two elements that contain colors for the real and imaginary 3D bars
alpha	Float containing desired transparency for the 3D bars

Using the plot_bloch_multivector Function

The `plot_bloch_multivector()` function takes a statevector or density matrix and represents it on one or more Bloch spheres. We'll demonstrate this function in Example 3-4 by plotting the statevector from a circuit containing a QFT.

Example 3-4. Using the `plot_bloch_multivector()` function to plot a statevector

```
from qiskit import QuantumCircuit,Aer,transpile
from qiskit.visualization \
    import plot_bloch_multivector
from math import pi

backend = \
    Aer.get_backend("aer_simulator_statevector")

qc = QuantumCircuit(3)
qc.rx(pi, 0)
qc.ry(pi/8, 2)
qc.swap(0, 2)
qc.h(0)
qc.cp(pi/2,0, 1)
qc.cp(pi/4, 0, 2)
qc.h(1)
qc.cp(pi/2, 1, 2)
qc.h(2)
qc.save_statevector()

tqc = transpile(qc, backend)
job = backend.run(tqc)
result = job.result()
statevector = result.get_statevector()

plot_bloch_multivector(statevector)
```

Figure 3-4 shows one Bloch sphere for each qubit in a quantum state. Note that the arrow doesn't always reach the surface of the Bloch sphere, namely in cases where qubits are entangled or the state is a *mixed state* (see the mixed state example in "Using the DensityMatrix Class").

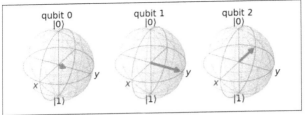

Figure 3-4. Example Bloch spheres produced by the plot_bloch_multivector() *function*

Table 3-4 shows commonly used plot_bloch_multivector parameters.

Table 3-4. Commonly used plot_bloch_multivector *parameters*

Parameter name	Description
state	Statevector, DensityMatrix, or ndarray (a NumPy type) containing complex numbers that represents a pure or mixed quantum state
title	A string to label the plot title
figsize	Tuple containing figure size in inches
reverse_bits	Boolean indicating whether to show the most significant Bloch sphere on the left

Using the plot_state_hinton Function

The plot_state_hinton() function takes a statevector or density matrix and represents it on a *Hinton diagram*. We'll demonstrate this function in Example 3-5 by plotting the density matrix from the *mixed state* example in "Using the Density-Matrix Class" on page 91.

Example 3-5. Using the plot_state_hinton() function to plot a density matrix for a mixed state

```
from qiskit.quantum_info import DensityMatrix, \
                                Operator
from qiskit.visualization import plot_state_hinton

dens_mat = 0.5*DensityMatrix.from_label('11') + \
  0.5*DensityMatrix.from_label('+0')
tt_op = Operator.from_label('TT')
dens_mat = dens_mat.evolve(tt_op)

plot_state_hinton(dens_mat)
```

Figure 3-5 shows a Hinton diagram that represents the complex numbers in the density matrix. The left half represents the real parts, and the right half represents the imaginary parts. See "Using the DensityMatrix Class" for a discussion on the *mixed state* in this example.

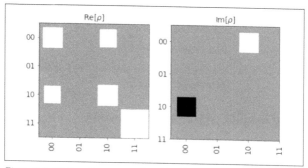

Figure 3-5. Hinton diagram produced by the plot_state_hinton() function

Table 3-5 contains a list of commonly used plot_state_hinton parameters.

Table 3-5. Commonly used `plot_state_hinton` *parameters*

Parameter name	Description
`state`	`Statevector`, `DensityMatrix`, or `ndarray` (a NumPy type) containing complex numbers that represents a pure or mixed quantum state
`title`	A string to label the plot title
`figsize`	Tuple containing figure size in inches

Using the plot_state_paulivec Function

The `plot_state_paulivec()` function takes a statevector or density matrix and represents it as a sparse bar graph of *expectation values* over the Pauli matrices. We'll demonstrate this function in Example 3-6 by representing the density matrix from the *mixed state* example in "Using the DensityMatrix Class" on page 91.

Example 3-6. Using the `plot_state_paulivec()` *function to represent a density matrix for a mixed state*

```
from qiskit.quantum_info import DensityMatrix, \
                                Operator
from qiskit.visualization import plot_state_paulivec

dens_mat = 0.5*DensityMatrix.from_label('11') + \
  0.5*DensityMatrix.from_label('+0')
tt_op = Operator.from_label('TT')
dens_mat = dens_mat.evolve(tt_op)

plot_state_paulivec(dens_mat)
```

Figure 3-6 shows a sparse bar graph that represents the density matrix as expectation values over the Pauli matrices.

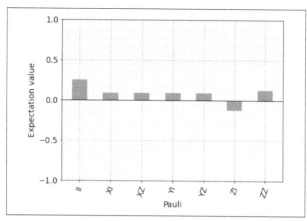

*Figure 3-6. Bar graph produced by the plot_state_paulivec()
function*

Table 3-6 lists commonly used plot_state_paulivec
parameters.

Table 3-6. Commonly used plot_state_paulivec parameters

Parameter name	Description
state	Statevector, DensityMatrix, or ndarray (a NymPy type) containing complex numbers that represents a pure or mixed quantum state
title	A string to label the plot title
figsize	Tuple containing figure size in inches
color	String or list of strings for the expectation value bar colors

## CHAPTER 4

Using the Transpiler

We've been using the `QuantumCircuit` class to represent quantum programs, and the purpose of quantum programs is to run them on real devices and get results from them. When programming, we usually don't worry about the device-specific details and instead use high-level operations. But most devices (and some simulators) can carry out only a small set of operations and can perform multiqubit gates only between certain qubits. This means we need to transpile our circuit for the specific device we're running on.

The transpilation process involves converting the operations in the circuit to those supported by the device and swapping qubits (via swap gates) within the circuit to overcome limited qubit connectivity. Qiskit's transpiler does this job, as well as some optimization to reduce the circuit's gate count where it can.

Quickstart with Transpile

In this section, we'll show you how to use the transpiler to get your circuit device-ready. We'll give a brief overview of the transpiler's logic and how we can get the best results from it.

The only required argument for transpile is the QuantumCircuit we want to transpile, but if we want transpile to do something interesting, we'll need to tell it what we want it to do. The easiest way to get your circuit running on a device is to simply pass transpile the backend object and let it grab the properties it needs. transpile returns a new QuantumCircuit object that is compatible with the backend. The following code snippet shows what the simplest usage of the transpiler looks like:

```
from qiskit import transpile
transpiled_circuit = transpile(circuit, backend)
```

For example, here we create a simple QuantumCircuit with one qubit, a YGate and two CXGates:

```
from qiskit import QuantumCircuit
qc = QuantumCircuit(3)
qc.y(0)
for t in range(2): qc.cx(0,t+1)
qc.draw()
```

Figure 4-1 shows the output of qc.draw().

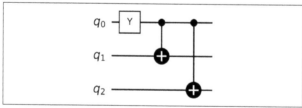

Figure 4-1. Simple circuit with a Y gate and two CX gates

In the next code snippet, we decide we want to run qc on the mock backend FakeSantiago (a mock backend contains the properties and noise models of a real system and uses the Aer Simulator to simulate that system). We can see in the output (shown after the code) that FakeSantiago doesn't understand the YGate operation:

```
from qiskit.test.mock import FakeSantiago
santiago = FakeSantiago()
santiago.configuration().basis_gates
```

```
['id', 'rz', 'sx', 'x', 'cx', 'reset']
```

So qc will need transpiling before running. In the next code snippet, we'll see what the transpiler does when we give it qc and tell it to transpile for santiago:

```
t_qc = transpile(qc, santiago)
t_qc.draw()
```

Figure 4-2 shows the output of t_qc.draw().

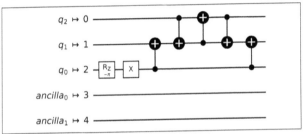

Figure 4-2. Result of transpiling a simple circuit

We can see in Figure 4-2 that the transpiler has done the following:

- Mapped (virtual) qubits 0, 1, and 2 in qc to (physical) qubits 2, 1, and 0 in t_qc, respectively
- Added three more CXGates to swap (physical) qubits 0 and 1
- Replaced our YGate with an RZGate and an XGate
- Added two extra qubits (as santiago has five qubits)

Most of this seems pretty reasonable, except the addition of all those CXGates. CXGates are generally quite expensive operations, so we want to avoid them as much as possible. So why has the transpiler done this? In some quantum systems, including santiago, not all qubits can communicate directly with one other.

We can check which qubits can talk to one other through that system's *coupling map* (run backend.configuration() .coupling_map to get this). A quick look at santiago's coupling map shows us that physical qubit 2 can't talk to physical qubit 0, so we need to add a swap somewhere.

Here is the output of santiago.configuration().coupling_map:

```
[[0, 1], [1, 0], [1, 2], [2, 1], [2, 3],
 [3, 2], [3, 4], [4, 3]]
```

When calling transpile, if we set initial_layout=[1,0,2], we can change the way qc maps to the backend and avoid unnecessary swaps. Here, the index of each element in the list represents the *virtual* qubit (in qc), and the value at that index represents the *physical* qubit. This improved layout overrides the transpiler's guess, and it doesn't need to insert any extra CXGates. The following code snippet shows this:

```
t_qc = transpile(qc, santiago, initial_layout=
                                        [1,0,2])
t_qc.draw()
```

Figure 4-3 shows the output of t_qc.draw() in the preceding code snippet.

As santiago has only five qubits, it was relatively easy to spot a good layout for this circuit on this device. For larger circuit/device combinations, we will want to do this algorithmically. One option is to set optimization_level=2 to ask the transpiler to use a smarter (but more expensive) algorithm to select a better layout.

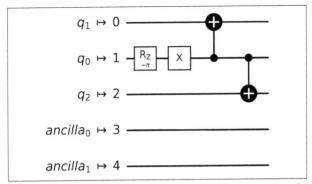

Figure 4-3. Result of transpiling a simple circuit with a smarter initial layout

The `transpile` function accepts four possible settings for `optimization_level`:

`optimization_level=0`

The transpiler simply does the absolute minimum necessary to get the circuit running on the backend. The initial layout keeps the indices of physical and virtual qubits the same, adds any swaps needed, and converts all gates to basis gates.

`optimization_level=1`

This is the default value. The transpiler makes smarter decisions. For example, if we have fewer virtual than physical qubits, the transpiler chooses the most well-connected subset of physical qubits and maps the virtual qubits to these. The transpiler also combines/removes sequences of gates where possible (e.g., two CXGates that cancel each other out).

`optimization_level=2`

The transpiler will search for an initial layout that doesn't need any swaps to execute the circuit or, failing this, go for the most well-connected subset of qubits. Like level 1, the transpiler also tries to collapse and cancel out gates where possible.

```
optimization_level=3
```
This is the highest value we can set. The transpiler will use smarter algorithms to cancel out gates in addition to the measures taken with `optimization_level=2`.

Transpiler Passes

Depending on your use case, the transpiler is often invisible. Functions like `execute` call it automatically, and thanks to the transpiler, we can usually ignore the specific device we're working on when creating circuits. Despite this low profile, the transpiler can have a huge effect on the performance of a circuit. In this section, we'll look at the decisions the transpiler makes and see how to change its behavior when we need to.

The PassManager

We build a transpilation routine from a bunch of smaller "passes." Each pass is a program that performs a small task (e.g., deciding the initial layout or inserting swap gates), and we use a `PassManager` object to organize our sequence of passes. In this section, we'll show a simple example using the `BasicSwap` pass.

First, we need a quantum circuit to transpile. The following code snippet creates a simple circuit we'll use as an example:

```
from qiskit import QuantumCircuit
qc = QuantumCircuit(3)
qc.h(0)
qc.cx(0, 2)
qc.cx(2, 1)
qc.draw()
```

Figure 4-4 shows the output of `qc.draw()`.

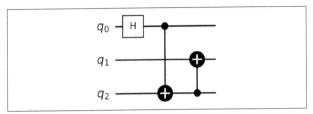

Figure 4-4. Simple circuit containing two CX gates

Next, we need to import and construct the PassManager and the passes we want to use. The BasicSwap constructor asks for the coupling map of the device we want to run our circuit on. In the following code snippet, we'll pretend we want to run this on a device in which qubit 0 can't interact with qubit 2 (but qubit 1 can interact with both). The PassManager constructor asks for the passes we want to apply to our circuit, which in this case is just the basic_swap pass we created in the preceding line:

```
from qiskit.transpiler import PassManager,
                                    CouplingMap
from qiskit.transpiler.passes import BasicSwap

coupling_map = CouplingMap([[0,1], [1,2]])
basic_swap_pass = BasicSwap(coupling_map)
pm = PassManager(basic_swap_pass)
```

Now that we've created our transpilation procedure, we can apply it to the circuit using the following code snippet:

```
routed_qc = pm.run(qc)
routed_qc.draw()
```

Figure 4-5 shows the output of routed_qc.draw().

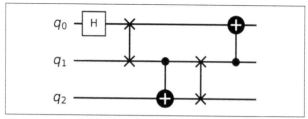

Figure 4-5. Simple circuit containing two CX gates and two swaps needed to execute on hardware

In Figure 4-5, we can see the basic_swap pass has added in two swap gates to carry out the CXGates, though note that it hasn't returned the qubits to their original order.

Compiling/Translating Passes

To get a circuit running on a device, we need to convert all the operations in our circuit to instructions the device supports. This can involve breaking high-level gates into lower-level gates (a form of compiling) or translating one set of low-level gates to another. Figure 4-6 shows how the transpiler might break a multicontrolled-X gate down to smaller gates.

Figure 4-6. Example of a multicontrolled-X gate decomposed into H, phase, and CX gates

At the time of writing, Qiskit has two ways of working out how to break a gate down into smaller gates. The first is through the gate's definition attribute. If set, this attribute contains a QuantumCircuit equal to that gate. The Decompose and Unroller passes both use this definition to expand circuits. The Decompose pass expands the circuit by only one level; i.e., it won't then try to decompose the definitions we replaced each gate with. The .decompose() method of the QuantumCircuit class uses the Decompose pass. The Unroller pass is similar, but it will continue decomposing the definitions of each gate recursively until the circuit contains only the basis gates we specify when we construct it.

The second way of breaking down gates is by consulting an `EquivalenceLibrary`. This library can store many definition circuits for each instruction, allowing passes to choose how to decompose each circuit. This has the advantage of not being tied to one specific set of basis gates. The `BasisTranslator` constructor needs an `EquivalenceLibrary` and a list of gate name labels. If the circuit contains gates *not* in the equivalence library, then we have no option but to use those gates' built-in definitions. The `UnrollCustomDefinitions` pass looks at the `EquivalenceLibrary`, and if each gate does not have an entry in the library, it unrolls that gate using its `.definition` attribute. In the preset transpiler routines (which we'll see later in this chapter), we'll usually see the `UnrollCustomDefinitions` pass immediately before the `BasisTranslator` pass.

Routing Passes

Some devices can perform multiqubit gates only between specific subsets of qubits. IBM's hardware tends to allow only one multiqubit gate (the `CXGate`) and can perform these gates only between specific pairs of qubits. We call a list of each pair of possible two-qubit interactions a *coupling map*. We saw an example of this in "The PassManager" on page 72. In that example, we overcame this limitation by using swap gates to move qubits around in the coupling map. Figure 4-7 shows an example of a coupling map.

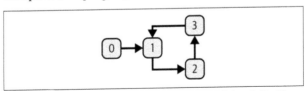

Figure 4-7. Drawing of a coupling map: [[0, 1], [1, 2], [2, 3], [3, 1]]

Qiskit has a few algorithms to add these swap gates. Table 4-1 lists each of the available swapping passes, with a brief description of the pass.

Table 4-1. Swapping transpiler passes available in Qiskit

Name	Explanation
BasicSwap	This pass does the least computational work needed to get the circuit running on the backend.
Lookahead Swap	Unlike BasicSwap, this pass uses a smarter algorithm to reduce the number of swap gates. It does a best-first search through all the potential combinations of swaps.
Stochas ticSwap	This is the swap pass used in the preset pass managers. This pass is not deterministic, so it might not produce the same circuit each time.
SabreSwap	This pass uses the SABRE (SWAP-based BidiREctional heuristic search) algorithm to try to reduce the number of swaps needed.
BIPMapping	This pass both solves the initial layout and swaps at the same time. The pass maps these problems to a BIP (Binary Integer Programming) problem, which it solves using external programs (docplex and CPLEX) you will need to install. Additionally, this pass does not cope well with large coupling maps (>~ 10 qubits).

Optimization Passes

The transpiler acts partly as a compiler, and like most compilers, it also includes some optimization passes. The biggest problem in modern quantum computers is noise, and the focus of these optimization passes is to reduce the noise in the output circuit as much as possible. Most of these optimization passes try to reduce noise and running time by minimizing gate count.

The simplest optimizations look for sequences of gates that have no effect, so we can safely remove them. For example, two CXGates back-to-back would have no effect on the unitary matrix of the circuit, so the CXCancellation pass removes them. Similarly, the RemoveDiagonalGatesBeforeMeasure pass does as it advertises and removes any gates with diagonal unitaries immediately before a measurement (as they won't change measurements in the computational basis). The OptimizeSwap BeforeMeasure pass removes SWAP gates immediately before a measurement and remaps the measurements to the classical register to preserve the output bit string.

Qiskit also has smarter optimization passes that attempt to replace groups of gates with smaller or more efficient groups of gates. For example, we can easily collect sequences of single-qubit gates and replace them with a single UGate, which we can then break back down into an efficient set of basis gates. The Optimize1qGates and Optimize1qGatesDecomposition passes both do this for different sets of initial gates. We can also do the same for two-qubit gates; Collect2qBlocks and Consol idateBlocks find sequences of two-qubit gates and compile them into one two-qubit unitary matrix. The UnitarySynthesis pass can then break this back down to the basis gates of our choosing.

For example, Figure 4-8 shows two circuits with identical unitaries but different numbers of gates.

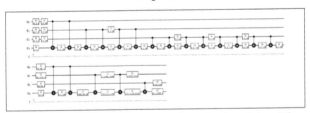

Figure 4-8. Example of the same circuit after going through two different transpilation processes

Initial Layout Selection Passes

As with routing, we also need to choose how to initially map our virtual circuit qubits to the physical device qubits. Table 4-2 lists some layout selection algorithms Qiskit offers.

Table 4-2. Initial layout transpiler passes available in Qiskit

Name	Explanation
Trivial Layout	This pass simply maps circuit qubits to physical qubits via their indexes. For example, the circuit qubit with index 3 will map to the device qubit with index 3.
Dense Layout	This pass finds the most well-connected group of physical qubits and maps the circuit qubits to this group.
Noise Adaptive Layout	This pass uses information about the device's noise properties to choose a layout.
Sabre Layout	This pass uses the SABRE algorithm to find an initial layout requiring as few SWAPs as possible.
CSPLayout	This pass converts layout selection to a constraint satisfaction problem (CSP). The pass then uses the constraint module's RecursiveBacktrackingSolver to try to find the best layout.

Preset PassManagers

When we used the high-level transpile function before, we didn't worry about the individual passes and instead set the optimization_level parameter. This parameter tells the transpiler to use one of four preset pass managers. Qiskit builds these preset pass managers through functions that take configuration settings and return a PassManager object. Now that we understand some passes, we can have a look at what the different transpilation routines are doing.

Following is the code we used to extract the passes used for a simple transpilation routine in case you want to reproduce it:

```python
from qiskit.transpiler import (PassManagerConfig,
                               CouplingMap)
from qiskit.transpiler.preset_passmanagers import\
                              level_0_pass_manager
from qiskit.test.mock import FakeSantiago

sys_conf = FakeSantiago().configuration()
pm_conf = PassManagerConfig(
    basis_gates=sys_conf.basis_gates,
    coupling_map=CouplingMap(sys_conf.coupling_map))

for i, step in enumerate(
    level_0_pass_manager(pm_conf).passes()):
    print(f'Step {i}:')
    for transpiler_pass in step['passes']:
        print(f'  {transpiler_pass.name()}')
```

We have not covered some of the following passes in this chapter because they are analysis passes that do not affect the circuit or because they are cleanup passes for which we don't have a choice of algorithm. These passes are unlikely to have an avoidable, negative effect on the performance of our circuits. We have also not covered some pulse-level passes that are out of the scope of this chapter:

```
Step 0:
  SetLayout
Step 1:
  TrivialLayout
Step 2:
  FullAncillaAllocation
  EnlargeWithAncilla
  ApplyLayout
Step 3:
  Unroll3qOrMore
Step 4:
  CheckMap
Step 5:
  BarrierBeforeFinalMeasurements
  StochasticSwap
Step 6:
  UnrollCustomDefinitions
```

```
    BasisTranslator
Step 7:
    TimeUnitConversion
Step 8:
    ValidatePulseGates
    AlignMeasures
```

Remember that optimization_level=0 does the bare minimum needed to get the circuit running on the device. Notably, we can see it uses TrivialLayout to choose an initial layout, then expands the circuit to have the same number of qubits as the device. The transpiler then unrolls the circuit to single and two-qubit gates and uses StochasticSwap for routing. Finally, it unrolls everything as far as possible and translates the circuit to the device's basis gates.

For optimization_level=3, on the other hand, the PassManager contains the following passes:

```
Step 0:
    Unroll3qOrMore
Step 1:
    RemoveResetInZeroState
    OptimizeSwapBeforeMeasure
    RemoveDiagonalGatesBeforeMeasure
Step 2:
    SetLayout
Step 3:
    TrivialLayout
    Layout2qDistance
Step 4:
    CSPLayout
Step 5:
    DenseLayout
Step 6:
    FullAncillaAllocation
    EnlargeWithAncilla
    ApplyLayout
Step 7:
    CheckMap
Step 8:
    BarrierBeforeFinalMeasurements
```

```
   StochasticSwap
Step 9:
  UnrollCustomDefinitions
  BasisTranslator
Step 10:
  RemoveResetInZeroState
Step 11:
  Depth
  FixedPoint
  Collect2qBlocks
  ConsolidateBlocks
  UnitarySynthesis
  Optimize1qGatesDecomposition
  CommutativeCancellation
  UnrollCustomDefinitions
  BasisTranslator
Step 12:
  TimeUnitConversion
Step 13:
  ValidatePulseGates
  AlignMeasures
```

This PassManager is quite different. After unrolling to single and two-qubit gates, we can already see some optimization passes in Step 1 removing unnecessary gates. The transpiler then tries a few different layout selection approaches. First, it checks if the TrivialLayout is optimal (i.e., if it doesn't need any SWAPs inserting to execute on the device). If it isn't, the transpiler then tries to find a layout using CSPLayout. If CSPLayout fails to find a solution, then the transpiler uses the DenseLayout algorithm. Next (Step 6), the transpiler adds extra qubits (if needed) to make the circuits have the same number of qubits as the device. It then uses the StochasticSwap algorithm to make all two-qubit gates possible on the device's coupling map. With the routing taken care of, the transpiler then translates the circuit to the device's basis gates before attempting some final optimizations in Step 11.

Looking at the optimization_level=3 passes, we can see that the transpiler is a very sophisticated program that can have a big influence on the behavior of your circuits. Fortunately, you now understand the problems the transpiler must solve and some of the algorithms it uses to solve them.

## PART II

Quantum Information and Algorithms

In fact, the mere act of opening the box will determine the state of the cat, although in this case there were three determinate states the cat could be in: these being Alive, Dead, and Bloody Furious.

—Terry Pratchett

In Part I, we explored the fundamentals of Qiskit, including creating and running quantum circuits and visualizing their results. Here in Part II, we'll discuss modules in Qiskit that leverage these fundamentals to apply quantum mechanical concepts to representing and processing information. We'll begin this journey by exploring quantum states, operators, channels, and measures in Chapter 5, "Quantum Information".

Then, we'll examine a module in Qiskit that facilitates expressing and manipulating quantum states and operations in Chapter 6, "Operator Flow".

Finally, we'll explore higher-level features of Qiskit that solve problems using algorithms that leverage the power of quantum information in Chapter 7, "Quantum Algorithms".

Quantum Information

The first three letters in the name Qiskit stand for *quantum information science*, which is the study of how quantum systems may be used to represent, process, and transmit information. The quantum_info module of Qiskit contains classes and functions that focus on those capabilities.

Using Quantum Information States

The qiskit.quantum_info module contains a few classes, shown in Table 5-1, that represent quantum information states.

Table 5-1. Classes that represent states in the `qiskit.quantum_info` module

Class name	Description
Statevector	Represents a statevector
DensityMatrix	Represents a density matrix
StabilizerState	Simulation of stabilizer circuits

We'll focus on the two most commonly used of these, namely the Statevector and DensityMatrix classes.

Using the Statevector Class

The Statevector class represents a quantum statevector and contains functionality for initializing and operating on the statevector. For example, as shown in the following code snippet, a Statevector may be instantiated by passing in a Quantum Circuit instance:

```
from qiskit import QuantumCircuit
from qiskit.quantum_info import Statevector

qc = QuantumCircuit(2)
qc.h(0)
qc.cx(0, 1)

statevector = Statevector(qc)
print(statevector.data)

output:
   [0.70710678+0.j 0.+0.j 0.+0.j 0.7071+0.j]
```

Notice that instead of running the circuit on a quantum simulator to get the statevector (as shown in the code in "Using the AerSimulator to calculate and hold a statevector" on page 44), we simply create an instance of Statevector with the desired QuantumCircuit.

Another way of creating a Statevector is to pass in a normalized complex vector, as shown in the following code snippet:

```
import numpy as np
from qiskit.quantum_info import Statevector

statevector = \
  Statevector([1, 0, 0, 1] / np.sqrt(2))
print(statevector.data)

output:
   [0.70710678+0.j 0.+0.j 0.+0.j 0.7071+0.j]
```

Yet another way of creating a Statevector is to pass a string of eigenstate ket labels to the from_label method, as shown in the following code snippet:

```
from qiskit.quantum_info import Statevector

statevector = Statevector.from_label('01-')
print(statevector.data)

output:
  [0.+0.j  0.+0.j  0.70710678+0.j -0.70710678+0.j
   0.+0.j  0.+0.j  0.+0.j  0.+0.j]
```

Tables 5-2 and 5-3 describe some of the methods and attributes in the Statevector class.

Table 5-2. Some Statevector methods

Method name	Description
conjugate	Returns the complex conjugate of the Statevector.
copy	Creates and returns a copy of the Statevector.
dims	Returns a tuple of dimensions.
draw	Returns a visualization of the Statevector, given the desired output method from the following: *text, latex, latex_source, qsphere, hinton, bloch, city,* or *paulivec.* Also see Chapter 3.
equiv	Returns a Boolean indicating whether a supplied State vector is equivalent to this one, up to a global phase.
evolve	Returns a quantum state evolved by the supplied operator. Also see "Using Quantum Information Operators" on page 95.
expand	Returns the reverse-order tensor product state of this Statevector and a supplied Statevector.
expectation_ value	Computes and returns the expectation value of a supplied operator.
from_ instruction	Returns the Statevector output of a supplied Instruction or QuantumCircuit instance.

Method name	Description
from_label	Instantiates a Statevector given a string of eigenstate ket labels. Each ket label may be 0, 1, +, -, r, or l and correspond to the six states found on the X-, Y-, and Z-axes of a Bloch sphere.
inner	Returns the inner product of this Statevector and a supplied Statevector.
is_valid	Returns a Boolean indicating whether this Statevector has norm 1.
measure	Returns the measurement outcome as well as post-measure state.
probabilities	Returns the measurement probability vector.
probabilities_dict	Returns the measurement probability dictionary.
purity	Returns a number from 0 to 1 indicating the purity of this quantum state. 1.0 indicates that this Statevector represents a pure quantum state.
reset	Resets to the 0 state.
reverse_qargs	Returns a Statevector with reversed basis state ordering.
sample_counts	Samples the probability distribution a supplied number of times, returning a dictionary of the counts.
sample_memory	Samples the probability distribution a supplied number of times, returning a list of the measurement results.
seed	Sets the seed for the quantum state random number generator.
tensor	Returns the tensor product state of this Statevector and a supplied Statevector.
to_dict	Returns the Statevector as a dictionary.

Method name	Description
to_operator	Returns a rank-1 projector operator by taking the outer product of the Statevector with its complex conjugate.
trace	Returns the trace of the quantum state as if it were represented as a density matrix. Also see "Using the DensityMatrix Class" on page 91.

Table 5-3. Some Statevector attributes

Attribute name	Description
data	Contains the complex vector
dim	Contains the number of basis states in the statevector
num_qubits	Contains the number of qubits in the statevector, or None

Example of using Statevector methods

As an example of using some of these Statevector methods and attributes, we'll first use the from_label method to create a Statevector whose basis states have equal probabilities of being the result of a measurement:

```
from qiskit.quantum_info import Statevector

statevector = Statevector.from_label('+-')
print(statevector.data)

output:
  [ 0.5+0.j -0.5+0.j  0.5+0.j -0.5+0.j]
```

We'll then use the draw method to visualize the statevector as the Q-sphere shown in Figure 5-1:

```
statevector.draw("qsphere")
```

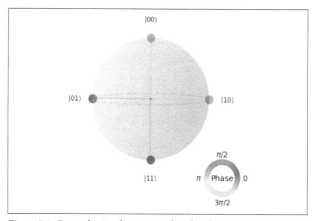

Figure 5-1. Example visualization produced with Statevector draw("qsphere")

Next, we'll use the probabilities method to show the probabilities of each basis state being the result of a measurement:

```
print(statevector.probabilities())

output:
  [0.25 0.25 0.25 0.25]
```

Finally, we'll use the sample_counts method to sample the probability distribution as if the circuit were being measured one thousand times:

```
print(statevector.sample_counts(1000))

output:
  {'00': 241, '01': 229, '10': 283, '11': 247}
```

Using the DensityMatrix Class

The `DensityMatrix` class represents a quantum density matrix and contains functionality for initializing and operating on the density matrix. For example, as shown in the following code snippet, a `DensityMatrix` may be instantiated by passing in a `QuantumCircuit` instance:

```
from qiskit import QuantumCircuit
from qiskit.quantum_info import DensityMatrix

qc = QuantumCircuit(2)
qc.h(0)
qc.cx(0, 1)
qc.z(1)

dens_mat = DensityMatrix(qc)
print(dens_mat.data)

output:
  [[ 0.5+0.j  0. +0.j  0. +0.j -0.5+0.j]
   [ 0. +0.j  0. +0.j  0. +0.j  0. +0.j]
   [ 0. +0.j  0. +0.j  0. +0.j  0. +0.j]
   [-0.5+0.j  0. +0.j  0. +0.j  0.5+0.j]]
```

Notice that the `DensityMatrix` contains a complex matrix, as opposed to the `Statevector`, which contains a complex vector. This enables the `DensityMatrix` to represent *mixed states*, which are an ensemble of two or more quantum states.

Tables 5-4 and 5-5 describe some of the methods and attributes in the `DensityMatrix` class.

Table 5-4. Some DensityMatrix methods

Method name	Description
conjugate	Returns the complex conjugate of the density matrix.
copy	Creates and returns a copy of the density matrix.
dims	Returns a tuple of dimensions.

Method name	Description
draw	Returns a visualization of the `DensityMatrix`, given the desired output method from the following: *text*, *latex*, *latex_source*, *qsphere*, *hinton*, *bloch*, *city*, or *paulivec*. Also see Chapter 3.
evolve	Returns a quantum state evolved by the supplied operator. Also see "Using Quantum Information Operators" on page 95.
expand	Returns the reverse-order tensor product state of this density matrix and a supplied `DensityMatrix`.
expecta tion_value	Computes and returns the expectation value of a supplied operator.
from_instruc tion	Returns the `DensityMatrix` output of a supplied `Instruction` or `QuantumCircuit` instance.
from_label	Instantiates a `DensityMatrix` given a string of eigenstate ket labels. Each ket label may be 0, 1, +, -, r, or l and correspond to the six states found on the X-, Y-, and Z-axes of a Bloch sphere.
is_valid	Returns a Boolean indicating whether this density matrix has trace 1 and is positive semidefinite.
measure	Returns the measurement outcome as well as post-measure state.
probabilities	Returns the measurement probability vector.
probabili ties_dict	Returns the measurement probability dictionary.
purity	Returns a number from 0 to 1 indicating the purity of this quantum state. 1.0 indicates that this density matrix represents a pure quantum state.
reset	Resets to the 0 state.
reverse_qargs	Returns a `DensityMatrix` with reversed basis state ordering.

Method name	Description
sample_counts	Samples the probability distribution a supplied number of times, returning a dictionary of the counts.
sample_memory	Samples the probability distribution a supplied number of times, returning a list of the measurement results.
seed	Sets the seed for the quantum state random number generator.
tensor	Returns the tensor product state of this density matrix and a supplied DensityMatrix.
to_dict	Returns the density matrix as a dictionary.
to_operator	Returns an operator converted from the density matrix.
to_statevector	Returns a Statevector from a pure density matrix.
trace	Returns the trace of the density matrix.

Table 5-5. Some DensityMatrix attributes

Attribute name	Description
data	Contains the complex matrix
dim	Contains the number of basis states in the density matrix
num_qubits	Contains the number of qubits in the density matrix, or none

Example of using DensityMatrix methods

As an example of using some of these DensityMatrix methods and attributes, we'll first create a mixed state by combining two density matrices, each of which is instantiated using the from_label method:

```
from qiskit.quantum_info import DensityMatrix, \
                                 Operator

dens_mat = 0.5*DensityMatrix.from_label('11') + \
  0.5*DensityMatrix.from_label('+0')
print(dens_mat.data)
```

```
output:
    [[0.25+0.j   0.+0.j   0.25+0.j   0.+0.j]
     [0.+0.j     0.+0.j   0.+0.j     0.+0.j]
     [0.25+0.j   0.+0.j   0.25+0.j   0.+0.j]
     [0.+0.j     0.+0.j   0.+0.j     0.5+0.j]]
```

Next we'll use the evolve method to evolve the state with an operator (see "Using Quantum Information Operators" on page 95). We'll then use the draw method to visualize the density matrix as the city plot shown in Figure 5-2:

```
tt_op = Operator.from_label('TT')
dens_mat = dens_mat.evolve(tt_op)
dens_mat.draw('city')
```

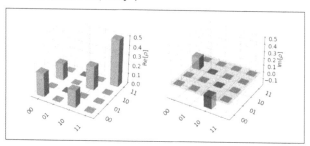

Figure 5-2. Example visualization produced by the DensityMatrix draw method

Next, we'll use the probabilities method to show the probabilities of each basis state being the result of a measurement:

```
print(dens_mat.probabilities())
```

```
output:
    [0.25 0.0 0.25 0.5]
```

Finally, we'll use the sample_counts method to sample the probability distribution as if the circuit were being measured one thousand times:

```
print(dens_mat.sample_counts(1000))
```

```
output:
  {'00': 240, '10': 256, '11': 504}
```

Using Quantum Information Operators

The `qiskit.quantum_info` module contains a few classes (see Table 5-6) that represent quantum information operators.

Table 5-6. Classes that represent operators in the `qiskit.quantum_info` module

Class name	Description
Operator	Operator class modeled with a complex matrix
Pauli	Multiqubit Pauli operator
Clifford	Multiqubit unitary operator from the Clifford group
ScalarOp	Scalar identity operator class
SparsePauliOp	Sparse multiqubit operator in a Pauli basis representation
CNOTDihedral	Multiqubit operator from the CNOT-Dihedral group
PauliList	List of multiqubit Pauli operators

We'll focus on the two most commonly used classes, namely the Operator and Pauli classes.

Using the Operator Class

The Operator class represents a quantum information operator, modeled by a matrix. For example, an Operator instance was used to evolve the quantum state represented by a Density Matrix in "Example of using DensityMatrix methods" on page 93. Operators are used in many ways, including by being placed into a QuantumCircuit with the append method discussed in "Using the append() method" on page 14.

An Operator may be instantiated in several ways, one of which is by passing in a QuantumCircuit instance, as shown in the following code snippet:

```python
from qiskit import QuantumCircuit
from qiskit.quantum_info import Operator

qc = QuantumCircuit(2)
qc.id(0)
qc.x(1)

op_XI = Operator(qc)
print(op_XI.data)
```

output:
```
  [[0.+0.j 0.+0.j 1.+0.j 0.+0.j]
   [0.+0.j 0.+0.j 0.+0.j 1.+0.j]
   [1.+0.j 0.+0.j 0.+0.j 0.+0.j]
   [0.+0.j 1.+0.j 0.+0.j 0.+0.j]]
```

Notice that the matrix for the operator is the unitary matrix for
the circuit. This technique may be used to obtain a unitary for
a circuit without running it on a quantum simulator (as shown
in the code in "Using the AerSimulator to calculate and hold a
unitary" on page 45).

Another way of creating an Operator is to pass in the desired
complex matrix, as shown in the following listing:

```python
from qiskit.quantum_info import Operator

op_XI = Operator([[0, 0, 1, 0],
                  [0, 0, 0, 1],
                  [1, 0, 0, 0],
                  [0, 1, 0, 0]])
print(op_XI.data)
```

output:
```
  [[0.+0.j 0.+0.j 1.+0.j 0.+0.j]
   [0.+0.j 0.+0.j 0.+0.j 1.+0.j]
   [1.+0.j 0.+0.j 0.+0.j 0.+0.j]
   [0.+0.j 1.+0.j 0.+0.j 0.+0.j]]
```

Yet another way of creating an Operator is to pass a Pauli
instance (see "Using the Pauli Class" on page 99):

```
from qiskit.quantum_info import Operator, Pauli

op_XI = Operator(Pauli('XI'))
print(op_XI.data)

output:
  [[0.+0.j 0.+0.j 1.+0.j 0.+0.j]
   [0.+0.j 0.+0.j 0.+0.j 1.+0.j]
   [1.+0.j 0.+0.j 0.+0.j 0.+0.j]
   [0.+0.j 1.+0.j 0.+0.j 0.+0.j]]
```

Notice that the three previous examples defined the same operator because their underlying matrices are identical. An additional way of creating an Operator is to pass an Instruction or Gate object (see "Instructions and Gates" on page 26), as shown in the following code snippet:

```
from qiskit.quantum_info import Operator
from qiskit.circuit.library.standard_gates \
                          import CPhaseGate
import numpy as np

op_CP = Operator(CPhaseGate(np.pi / 4))
print(op_CP.data)

output:
  [[1.+0.j 0.+0.j 0.+0.j 0.+0.j]
   [0.+0.j 1.+0.j 0.+0.j 0.+0.j]
   [0.+0.j 0.+0.j 1.+0.j 0.+0.j]
   [0.+0.j 0.+0.j 0.+0.j 0.70710678+0.70710678j]]
```

The CPhaseGate used in the previous example may be seen in "CPhaseGate" on page 159.

Tables 5-7 and 5-8 describe some of the methods and attributes in the Operator class.

Table 5-7. Some `Operator` methods

Method name	Description
adjoint	Returns the adjoint of the operator
compose	Returns the result of left-multiplying this operator with a supplied Operator
conjugate	Returns the complex conjugate of the operator
copy	Returns a copy of the Operator
dot	Returns the result of right-multiplying this operator with a supplied Operator
equiv	Returns a Boolean indicating whether a supplied Operator is equivalent to this one, up to a global phase
expand	Returns the reverse-order tensor product with another Operator
from_label	Returns a tensor product of single-qubit operators among the following: I, X, Y, Z, H, S, T, 0, 1, +, -, r, and l
is_unitary	Returns a Boolean indicating whether this operator is a unitary matrix
power	Returns an Operator raised to the supplied power
tensor	Returns the tensor product with another Operator
to_instruction	Returns this operator converted to a UnitaryGate
transpose	Returns the transpose of the operator

Table 5-8. Some `Operator` attributes

Attribute name	Description
data	Contains the operator's complex matrix
dim	Contains the dimensions of the operator's complex matrix
num_qubits	Contains the number of qubits in the operator, or None

Using the Pauli Class

The `Pauli` class represents a multiqubit Pauli operator in which each qubit is an X, Y, Z, or I Pauli matrix. A `Pauli` may be instantiated in several ways, the most common of which is to pass in a string containing Pauli operators preceded by an optional phase coefficient:

```
from qiskit.quantum_info import Pauli

pauli_piXZ = Pauli('-XZ')
print(pauli_piXZ.to_matrix())

output:
  [[ 0.+0.j  0.+0.j -1.+0.j  0.+0.j]
   [ 0.+0.j  0.+0.j  0.+0.j  1.-0.j]
   [-1.+0.j  0.+0.j  0.+0.j  0.+0.j]
   [ 0.+0.j  1.-0.j  0.+0.j  0.+0.j]]
```

Another way of creating a `Pauli` is to pass in a `QuantumCircuit` instance that contains only Pauli gates (X, Y, Z, I), as shown in the following code snippet:

```
from qiskit import QuantumCircuit
from qiskit.quantum_info import Pauli

qc = QuantumCircuit(2)
qc.z(0)
qc.x(1)

pauli_XZ = Pauli(qc)
print(pauli_XZ.equiv(Pauli('-XZ')))

output:
  True
```

Notice that the previous two examples produced equivalent Pauli operators, as they differ only by a global phase.

Tables 5-9 and 5-10 describe some of the methods and attributes in the `Pauli` class.

Table 5-9. Some `Pauli` methods

Method name	Description
adjoint	Returns the adjoint of the Pauli
commutes	Returns a Boolean indicating whether a supplied Pauli commutes with this one
compose	Returns the result of left-multiplying this Pauli with a supplied Pauli.
conjugate	Returns the complex conjugate of the Pauli
copy	Returns a copy of the Pauli
dot	Returns the result of right-multiplying this Pauli with a supplied Pauli
equiv	Returns a Boolean indicating whether a supplied Pauli is equivalent to this one, up to a global phase
expand	Returns the reverse-order tensor product with another Pauli
inverse	Returns the inverse of the Pauli
power	Returns a Pauli raised to the supplied power
tensor	Returns the tensor product with another Pauli
to_label	Returns this Pauli converted to string label containing an optional phase, and Pauli gates X, Y, Z, and I
to_matrix	Returns this Pauli as a complex matrix
transpose	Returns the transpose of the Pauli

Table 5-10. Some `Pauli` attributes

Attribute name	Description
dim	Contains the dimensions of the complex Pauli matrix
num_qubits	Contains the number of qubits in the Pauli, or None
phase	Contains an integer that represent the phase of the Pauli

Using Quantum Information Channels

The qiskit.quantum_info module contains a few classes, shown in Table 5-11, that represent quantum information channels.

Table 5-11. Classes that represent channels in the `qiskit.quantum_info` module

Class name	Description
Choi	Choi-matrix representation of a quantum channel
SuperOp	Superoperator representation of a quantum channel
Kraus	Kraus representation of a quantum channel
Stinespring	Stinespring representation of a quantum channel
Chi	Pauli basis Chi-matrix representation of a quantum channel
PTM	Pauli Transfer Matrix (PTM) representation of a quantum channel

We'll focus on a representative sample of these, namely the Kraus class, to model a noisy quantum channel whose qubits flip about 10% of the time. In the following code snippet, a Kraus instance is created with a matrix that models this bit-flip behavior and is appended to a quantum circuit:

```python
from qiskit import QuantumCircuit
from qiskit.quantum_info import Kraus
import numpy as np

noise_ops = [np.sqrt(0.9) * np.array([[1, 0],
                                      [0, 1]]),
             np.sqrt(0.1) * np.array([[0, 1],
                                      [1, 0]])]
kraus = Kraus(noise_ops)

qc = QuantumCircuit(2)
qc.append(kraus, [0])
qc.append(kraus, [1])
```

```
qc.measure_all()
qc.draw()
```

The resulting circuit is shown in Figure 5-3.

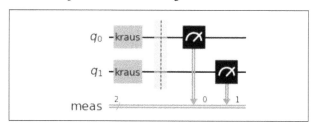

Figure 5-3. Example quantum circuit containing Kraus quantum channels

In the following code snippet, we'll use an aer_simulator (see "Using the AerSimulator to hold measurement results" on page 42) to run the circuit, followed by printing the measurement results:

```
from qiskit import Aer, transpile

backend = Aer.get_backend("aer_simulator")
tqc = transpile(qc, backend)
job = backend.run(tqc, shots=1000)
result = job.result()
counts = result.get_counts(tqc)
print(counts)

output:
  {'11': 8, '01': 90, '00': 818, '10': 84}
```

Notice that the measurements are approximately what would be expected from each qubit having a 0.1 probability of flipping.

Using Quantum Information Measures

The qiskit.quantum_info module contains several functions, shown in Table 5-12, that return various measurements values.

Table 5-12. Functions that return various measurement values in the qiskit.quantum_info module

Function name	Description
average_gate_fidelity	Returns the average gate fidelity of a noisy quantum channel
process_fidelity	Returns the process fidelity of a noisy quantum channel
gate_error	Returns the gate error of a noisy quantum channel
diamond_norm	Returns the diamond norm of the input quantum channel object
state_fidelity	Returns the state fidelity between two quantum states
purity	Returns the purity of a quantum state
concurrence	Returns the concurrence of a quantum state
entropy	Returns the von Neumann entropy of a quantum state
entanglement_of_formation	Returns the entanglement of formation of quantum state
mutual_information	Returns the mutual information of a bipartite state

We'll focus on one representative of these, namely the state_fidelity function.

Using the state_fidelity Function

The state_fidelity() function takes two Statevector or DensityMatrix instances and returns the state fidelity between them. In the following code snippet, the state fidelity of a one-qubit statevector in equal superposition has an 85% state fidelity with a statevector whose phase is subsequently rotated by π/8 radians:

```
from qiskit.quantum_info import Statevector, \
                    Operator, state_fidelity

sv_a = Statevector.from_label('+')
sv_b = sv_a.evolve(Operator.from_label('T'))
print(state_fidelity(sv_a, sv_b))

output:
  0.8535533905932733
```

## CHAPTER 6

Operator Flow

The `qiskit.opflow` module contains classes for expressing and manipulating quantum states and operations. Some of the functionality is backed by classes in the `qiskit.quantum_info` module. One of the main purposes of this Operator Flow layer is to facilitate the development of quantum algorithms.

Creating Operator Flow Expressions

The `qiskit.opflow` module contains an immutable set of operators, shown in Table 6-1, that are useful in creating expressions that contain quantum states and operators.

Table 6-1. Immutable operators in the `qiskit.opflow` module

Operator	Description
X	Pauli X
Y	Pauli Y
Z	Pauli Z
I	Pauli I
H	H gate
S	S gate

Operator	Description
T	T gate
CX	CX gate
CZ	CZ gate
Swap	SWAP gate
Zero	Qubit 0 state
One	Qubit 1 state
Plus	Qubit + state
Minus	Qubit - state

In order to use these operators in expressions, we'll need algebraic operations and predicates, such as those shown in Table 6-2.

Table 6-2. Algebraic operations and predicates in the `qiskit.opflow` *module*

Algebraic operation	Description
+	Addition
-	Subtraction/negation
*	Scalar multiplication
/	Scalar division
@	Composition
^	Tensor product or tensor power
**	Composition power
==	Equality
~	Adjoint

These algebraic operations are syntactic sugar for underlying methods that perform functions such as computing tensor products and multiplying matrices, which allows representing complex formulas with a concise syntax.

Using operators and algebraic operations from Tables 6-1 and 6-2 we can create expressions such as the arbitrary state $|10010\rangle$ in the following code snippet. As with other examples in this book, and in Qiskit as a whole, the least significant qubit is represented by the rightmost binary digit:

```
from qiskit.opflow import Zero, One

state = One ^ Zero ^ One ^ Zero ^ Zero
print(state)

output:
  DictStateFn({'10100': 1})
```

Notice that the output reveals the class, DictStateFn, in which our state is held. We'll explore these classes soon.

We can also create expressions such as the arbitrary Pauli operator with a phase coefficient in the following listing:

```
from qiskit.opflow import X, Z

pauli_piXZ = -(X ^ Z)
print(pauli_piXZ)

output:
  -1.0 * XZ
```

You may recognize this Pauli operator as an example used in "Using the Pauli Class" on page 99. In that example, the matrix that models the operator was printed, and we'll do so here to show that it is the same:

```
print(pauli_piXZ.to_matrix())

output:
  [[-0.+0.j -0.+0.j -1.+0.j -0.+0.j]
   [-0.+0.j -0.+0.j -0.+0.j  1.-0.j]
   [-1.+0.j -0.+0.j -0.+0.j -0.+0.j]
   [-0.+0.j  1.-0.j -0.+0.j -0.+0.j]]
```

Now we'll create an Operator Flow expression that represents a GHZ circuit:

```python
from qiskit.opflow import I, X, H, CX

op = (CX ^ I) @ (I ^ CX) @ (I ^ I ^ H)
print(op)
```

output:

Notice that Operator Flow notation is little-endian. For example, the H gate in the expression is placed on the least significant qubit wire. Also notice that the control wire of a given CX gate is on the lesser index of its qubit wires.

For fun, let's convert the expression to a circuit and sample the probability distribution using a `Statevector` (see "Using the Statevector Class" on page 86):

```python
from qiskit.quantum_info import Statevector

qc = op.to_circuit()
sv = Statevector(qc)
print(sv.sample_counts(1000))
```

output:
  {'000': 482, '111': 518}

Underlying this Operator Flow expression syntax is a rich set of classes for representing states, operators, and other constructs. Let's dive into how Operator Flow represents states, with the state function classes.

Using the Operator Flow State Function Classes

The `qiskit.opflow.state_fns` module contains a few classes, shown in Table 6-3, that represent state functions.

Table 6-3. Some classes that represent state functions in the `qiskit.opflow.state_fns` *module*

Class name	Description
StateFn	Base class and factory for StateFn subclasses.
Circuit StateFn	Represents a state function, backed by a Quantum Circuit instance that assumes all-zero qubit inputs. See "Constructing Quantum Circuits" on page 3.
DictStateFn	Represents a state function, backed by a Python dictionary.
Vector StateFn	Represents a state function, backed by a Statevector class. See "Using the Statevector Class" on page 86.
SparseVec torStateFn	Contains a sparse representation of a state function.
Operator StateFn	Represents a state function, backed by a density operator.

We'll focus on the `StateFn` class, which is the base class and factory for the rest of these classes.

Using the StateFn Class

The `StateFn` class is the base class for all the state function classes in Operator Flow. This class also serves as a factory for these state function classes in Operator Flow. For example, as shown in the following listing, a `DictStateFn` may be instantiated by passing a bit string into a `StateFn`:

```
from qiskit.opflow.state_fns import StateFn

statefn = StateFn('10100')
print(statefn)
```

```
output:
  DictStateFn({'10100': 1})
```

Notice that this creates an instance of the same class, Dict StateFn, as when using an Operator Flow expression to create that state function in "Creating Operator Flow Expressions" on page 105.

For another example, as shown in the following code, a Circuit StateFn may be instantiated by passing a QuantumCircuit into a StateFn:

```
from qiskit import QuantumCircuit

qc = QuantumCircuit(3)
qc.h(0)
qc.cx(0, 1)
qc.cx(1, 2)

statefn = StateFn(qc)
print(statefn)

output:
  CircuitStateFn(
```

```
  )
```

This creates an instance of the same class, CircuitStateFn, as when using an Operator Flow expression to create a GHZ state in "Creating Operator Flow Expressions".

For yet another example, as shown in the following listing, a VectorStateFn may be instantiated by passing a list of amplitudes into a StateFn:

```
import numpy as np
```

```
statefn = StateFn([1, 0, 0, 1] / np.sqrt(2))
print(statefn)

output:
  VectorStateFn(Statevector([
                0.70710678+0.j,
                0.+0.j,
                0.+0.j,
                0.70710678+0.j],
            dims=(2, 2)))
```

Note that this creates an instance of `Statevector`, just as we did with a similar example in "Using the Statevector Class" on page 86.

Tables 6-4, 6-5 and 6-6 describe some of the instantiation parameters, methods, and attributes in the `StateFn` class.

Table 6-4. Some StateFn instantiation parameters

Parameter name	Description
primitive	Determines which of the StateFn classes will be created, and sets its initial value. Can be either a str, dict, Result, list, ndarray, Statevector, QuantumCircuit, Instruction, OperatorBase, or None.
coeff	Coefficient of this state function.
is_meas urement	If True, this state function is to be a bra (row vector) rather than a ket (column vector).

Supplying a `True` `is_measurement` argument is related to using the ~ (adjoint) algebraic operator from Table 6-2. In the following example, the values of `statefn_a` and `statefn_b` are equivalent:

```
from qiskit.opflow.state_fns import StateFn
from qiskit.opflow import One, Zero

statefn_a = StateFn('100', is_measurement=True)
print('statefn_a:', statefn_a,
      statefn_a.is_measurement)
```

```
statefn_b = ~(One ^ Zero ^ Zero)
print('statefn_b:', statefn_b,
      statefn_b.is_measurement)

output:
  statefn_a: DictMeasurement({'100': 1}) True
  statefn_b: DictMeasurement({'100': 1}) True
```

Note that the DictMeasurement in the output indicates that
is_measurement is True.

Table 6-5. Some StateFn methods

Method name	Description
add	Returns the addition of a supplied StateFn to this one. This is equivalent to using the + algebraic operator in Table 6-2.
adjoint	Returns the adjoint (complex conjugate) of this StateFn. This is equivalent to using the ~ algebraic operator in Table 6-2.
equals	Returns a Boolean that indicates whether the supplied StateFn is equal to this one up to global phase. This is equivalent to using the == algebraic operator in Table 6-2.
eval	Evaluates the underlying function of this StateFn.
mul	Returns the scalar multiplication of a supplied number to this StateFn. Number should be a valid int, float, complex, or Parameter instance. This is equivalent to using the * algebraic operator in Table 6-2.
primitive _strings	Return a set of strings describing the primitives contained in this StateFn.
sample	Samples the normalized probability distribution of this StateFn a supplied number of shots and returns a dictionary with the results.
tensor	Returns the tensor product of this StateFn with a supplied StateFn. This is equivalent to using the ^ algebraic operator in Table 6-2.

Method name	Description
tensorpower	Returns the tensor product of this StateFn with itself a supplied number of times, represented as an int. This is equivalent to using the ^ algebraic operator in Table 6-2.
to_circuit_op	Returns a CircuitOp that is equivalent to this StateFn.
to_density _matrix	Returns a matrix representing the product of StateFn evaluated on pairs of basis states.
to_matrix	Returns the NumPy representation of this StateFn.
to_matrix_op	Returns a VectorStateFn for this StateFn.

Table 6-6. Some Statevector attributes

Attribute name	Description
coeff	Coefficient of this state function.
is_measure ment	If True, this state function represents a bra (row vector) rather than a ket (column vector).
num_qubits	Contains the number of qubits in the state function.
primitive	Which of the StateFn classes implements the behavior of this state function.

Let's turn our attention to how Operator Flow represents operators, with the primitive operators classes.

Using the Operator Flow Primitive Operators Classes

The qiskit.opflow.primitive_ops module contains a few classes, shown in Table 6-7, that represent primitive operators.

Table 6-7. Some classes that represent primitive operators in the qiskit.opflow.primitive_ops module

Class name	Description
PrimitiveOp	Base class and factory for PrimitiveOp subclasses.

Class name	Description
CircuitOp	Represents a quantum operator, backed by a Quantum Circuit instance. See "Constructing Quantum Circuits" on page 3.
MatrixOp	Represents a quantum operator, backed by an Operator instance. See "Using the Operator Class" on page 95.
PauliOp	Represents a quantum operator, backed by a Pauli class. See "Using the Pauli Class" on page 99.

We'll focus on the PrimitiveOp class, which is the base class and factory for the rest of these classes.

Using the PrimitiveOp Class

The PrimitiveOp class is the base class for all of the primitive operator classes in Operator Flow. This class also serves as a factory for these classes. For example, as shown in the following listing, a PauliOp may be instantiated by passing a Pauli instance into a PrimitiveOp:

```
from qiskit.opflow.primitive_ops \
  import PrimitiveOp
from qiskit.quantum_info import Pauli

primop_piXZ = PrimitiveOp(Pauli('-XZ'))
print(primop_piXZ)
print(type(primop_piXZ))

output:
  -XZ
  <class '...PauliOp'>
```

Notice from the following code that this creates an instance of the same class, PauliOp, as when using an Operator Flow expression to create that primitive operator (see "Creating Operator Flow Expressions"). Also notice that the underlying primitives (the Pauli instances) are equivalent up to a global phase but that they are not equal, given that they are of different types:

```
from qiskit.opflow import X, Z

pauli_piXZ = -(X ^ Z)
print(type(pauli_piXZ))
print(primop_piXZ.primitive
      .equiv(pauli_piXZ.primitive))

output:
  <class '...PauliOp'>
  True
```

As shown in the following listing, a CircuitOp may be instantiated by passing a QuantumCircuit into a PrimitiveOp:

```
from qiskit import QuantumCircuit

qc = QuantumCircuit(3)
qc.h([0,1,2])

h_primop = PrimitiveOp(qc)
print(h_primop)
print(type(h_primop))

output:
```

```
    <class ...CircuitOp'>
```

This creates an instance of the same class, CircuitOp, as when using an Operator Flow expression to create the same circuit as shown in the following code:

```
from qiskit.opflow import H

hgates = H^3
print(hgates)
print(type(hgates))
```

```
output:
```

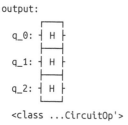

```
<class ...CircuitOp'>
```

Tables 6-8, 6-9, and 6-10 describe some of the instantiation parameters, methods, and attributes in the `PrimitiveOp` class.

Table 6-8. Some `PrimitiveOp` instantiation parameters

Parameter name	Description
primitive	Determines which of the `PrimitiveOp` classes will be created and sets its initial value. Can be either a `QuantumCircuit`, `Operator`, `Pauli`, `SparsePauliOp`, or `OperatorBase`.
coeff	Coefficient of this primitive operator

Table 6-9. Some `PrimitiveOp` methods

Method name	Description
add	Returns the addition of a supplied `PrimitiveOp` to this one. This is equivalent to using the + algebraic operator in Table 6-2.
adjoint	Returns the adjoint (complex conjugate) of this `PrimitiveOp`. This is equivalent to using the ~ algebraic operator in Table 6-2.
compose	Returns the operator composition of a supplied `PrimitiveOp` to this one. This is equivalent to using the @ algebraic operator in Table 6-2.
equals	Returns a Boolean that indicates whether the supplied `PrimitiveOp` is equal to this one. This is equivalent to using the == algebraic operator in Table 6-2.
eval	Evaluates the underlying function of this `PrimitiveOp`.

Method name	Description
exp_i	Returns the PrimitiveOp exponentiation.
mul	Returns the scalar multiplication of a supplied number to this PrimitiveOp. This is equivalent to using the * algebraic operator in Table 6-2.
primitive_ strings	Returns a set of strings describing the primitives contained in this PrimitiveOp.
tensor	Returns the tensor product of this PrimitiveOp with a supplied PrimitiveOp. This is equivalent to using the ^ algebraic operator in Table 6-2.
tensorpower	Returns the tensor product of this PrimitiveOp with itself a supplied number of times. This is equivalent to using the ^ algebraic operator in Table 6-2.
to_circuit_op	Returns a CircuitOp that is equivalent to this PrimitiveOp.
to_ instruction	Returns an Instruction equivalent to this PrimitiveOp.
to_matrix	Returns the NumPy representation of this Primitive Op.
to_matrix_op	Returns a MatrixOp for this PrimitiveOp.

Table 6-10. Some PrimitiveOp attributes

Attribute name	Description
coeff	Coefficient of this primitive operator
num_qubits	Contains the number of qubits in the primitive operator
primitive	Which of the PrimitiveOp classes implements the behavior of this primitive operator

## CHAPTER 7

Quantum Algorithms

Much like many sophisticated classical algorithms, in the future, we'd like to be able to run a quantum algorithm without knowing all the details about its implementation. Qiskit supports many popular quantum algorithms out of the box. You can simply specify a problem, then choose an algorithm to solve it. In this chapter, we'll explore Qiskit's algorithms module and the algorithms this module supports.

Background on Quantum Algorithms

Quantum algorithms are the motivation for most research and investment in quantum computing. The entire fields of quantum error correction, quantum hardware, and quantum software development (including Qiskit) ultimately work toward the common goal of running a useful algorithm on a quantum computer.

With this in mind, you might find it surprising that there are relatively few problems for which we think we could achieve *quantum advantage* (where a quantum computer outperforms modern classical computers). Finding new quantum algorithms and new ways to apply known algorithms is a very active area of research. Maybe even more surprising is that, of these candidate quantum algorithms, we're not actually sure some will have a speedup at all (never mind on huge, fault-tolerant computers). But why is this?

To guarantee a speedup over classical methods, we need to be able to directly compare the quantum algorithm to its classical counterpart, and to make a direct comparison, both algorithms must solve exactly the same problem. One consequence of this is that both algorithms must take classical data as an input and return classical data as an output. Some famous algorithms (e.g., Harrow, Hassidim, and Lloyd's algorithm, known as the *HHL algorithm*) take/return quantum superpositions as inputs and/or outputs and thus can't be directly compared to classical algorithms.

While algorithms with quantum inputs and outputs are still interesting in their own right, we can view them as building blocks, used as subroutines in other algorithms that *do* use classical inputs and outputs. Examples include Brassard, Høyer, and Tapp's quantum counting algorithm, which uses phase estimation as a subroutine, and Kerenidis and Prakash's recommendation algorithm, which they based on the HHL algorithm (more on this later).

If the quantum algorithm solves a classical problem, you can start to analyze how it behaves and use this to compare it to the best-known classical algorithm. For example, we know Shor's algorithm grows significantly slower than its best-known classical competitor, the general number field sieve, and this result is the reassurance many people needed to invest time and money into building quantum computers.

So far, we have been talking about comparisons to the "best-known" classical algorithms. The final step in proving that our quantum computer will *definitely* outperform a classical computer is to prove that no classical algorithm could possibly scale better than our quantum algorithm. As you might imagine, this is difficult to do.

Sometimes, the fact that many people have tried and failed to find an efficient classical algorithm counts as enough evidence that the quantum competitor is worth investing in, but the future sometimes surprises us. Previously, we mentioned Kerenidis and Prakash's recommendation algorithm, which was exponentially faster than the best-known classical algorithm for the same problem. Only three years later, Ewin Tang found a classical algorithm that was only polynomially slower than the quantum algorithm.

At the time of writing, we can already run simple quantum algorithms on real quantum hardware, and we are rapidly approaching the ability to test quantum algorithms empirically, instead of measuring their performance theoretically. As with classical computing, we will need to consider implementation details (not just the algorithm complexity) to ensure we get the best performance.

Using the Algorithms Module

All algorithm interfaces in Qiskit's algorithms module follow a consistent pattern. In this section, we'll learn about this general pattern and the rationale behind it.

Quickstart

First, let's see how we run a simple algorithm using Qiskit.

The code in the following snippet uses Qiskit's algorithms module to run Shor's algorithm on a simulator:

```
# Choose a backend to use
from qiskit.providers.aer import AerSimulator
aer_sim = AerSimulator()

# Create an instance of Shor's algorithm, using
# our backend
from qiskit.algorithms import Shor
shor = Shor(aer_sim)

# Execute algorithm on specific problem and
# view the result
```

```
result = shor.factor(21)
result.factors  # Has value: [[3, 7]]
```

We've split the preceding code snippet into three steps:

1. First, we need to choose a backend to run the algorithm on. Here, we've chosen the `AerSimulator`.

2. Next, we create an instance of Shor's algorithm using the backend.

3. We then run Shor's algorithm on the input `21` and view the results.

We can see that the `factors` attribute of `result` does contain the correct factors of 21.

The Algorithms Interface

When testing and researching different quantum algorithms, we want to be able to compare the performance of different algorithms (and variations on these algorithms) against the same problem.

The input to a factoring problem is always an integer, so Qiskit uses a Python `int` to represent a factoring problem. Other algorithms (e.g., amplitude amplification and amplitude estimation) have their own problem classes (e.g., `Amplification Problem` and `EstimationProblem`) that the algorithms will try to solve.

We can then compare the performance of different algorithms on these problem objects. For example, if we create an `EstimationProblem` object, Qiskit offers four different quantum algorithms to solve it:

- `AmplitudeEstimation`

- `FasterAmplitudeEstimation`

- `IterativeAmplitudeEstimation`

- `MaximumLikelihoodAmplitudeEstimation`

For other problems, Qiskit even incorporates some classical algorithms, such as `NumPyEigensolver`, `NumPyLinearSolver`, and `NumPyMinimumEigensolver`, so we can compare their results and performance.

If we view a quantum algorithm as a method of solving real-world problems, then we must also consider implementation details (e.g., the backend it runs on) as part of that method. When we construct the algorithm, we can specify the backend, as well as other device-specific implementation details, such as the transpiler `optimization_level`. These properties live inside a `QuantumInstance` object. For example, let's say we're using the default `AerSimulator`, which has no errors. This means we don't need to bother optimizing the circuits when we transpile them. In the following code snippet, we create a `QuantumInstance` with the `optimization_level` set to 0:

```
# Choose a backend to use
from qiskit.providers.aer import AerSimulator
aer_sim = AerSimulator()

# Construct the QuantumInstance with no
# optimization
from qiskit.utils import QuantumInstance
quantum_instance = QuantumInstance(
    aer_sim,
    optimization_level=0,
)
```

We can then use the following code snippet to construct and run Shor's algorithm using our `QuantumInstance` instead of a backend object:

```
from qiskit.algorithms import Shor
shor = Shor(quantum_instance)
result = shor.factor(15)
result.factors  # Has value: [[3, 5]]
```

As well as backend-specific parameters, we can also change algorithm-specific parameters. For example, the algorithm class `FasterAmplitudeEstimation` needs two parameters, one to specify the acceptable error and another to specify the maximum number of iterations allowed.

Traditional Quantum Algorithms

In this section, we'll cover the more traditional quantum algorithms in Qiskit's algorithms module and give a short example of each algorithm in action.

Grover's Algorithm

Grover's algorithm is one of the most famous quantum algorithms. Grover's is one of the few quantum algorithms that we can prove scales better than any possible classical algorithm, and it's actually provably optimal for quantum algorithms too. Figure 7-1 shows a high-level Grover circuit.

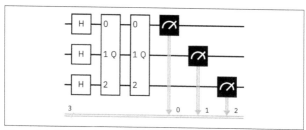

Figure 7-1. High-level example of Grover's algorithm, where Q is the Grover operator (discussed later in this section)

Grover's algorithm solves a specific case of the *amplification problem*: given two operators, A_θ and B_θ, that rotate around the states $|A\rangle$ and $|B\rangle$, create a circuit that transforms $|A\rangle$ into $|B\rangle$. Grover's specific case is where $|A\rangle$ is the superposition of all computational basis states and $|B\rangle$ is a specific computational basis state.

If we know how to create a program to check a solution to a problem, it's relatively straightforward to create a circuit that transforms around that solution's computational basis state (i.e., it's straightforward to create B_θ). This makes Grover's algorithm very widely applicable.

To use Grover's algorithm, we first need to specify the problem, which we do via the `AmplificationProblem` class. The `Amplifi cationProblem` constructor requires two arguments: the `oracle`, which is the `QuantumCircuit` that carries out the operator B_θ, and the `is_good_state` function, which takes a bit string and returns `True` if it's a solution.

In the following code snippet, we use the `PhaseOracle` class from Qiskit's circuit library to create an oracle from a simple Boolean expression.

Let's imagine that two parents, A and B, and their child, C, have two tickets for a play. Each person can either (0) not go to the play or (1) go to the play. At least one adult needs to go, so we have the requirement (A | B), where | is a Boolean OR. The other problem is that there are only two tickets, so we can't have all three going together. In our notation, this is ~(A & B & C), where ~ is the Boolean NOT and & is the Boolean AND. Finally, C particularly wants to go with B as C doesn't see B much during the week, so we have the added constraint of (B & C). Can we satisfy all these constraints?

You may have already worked out that the answer is *yes* and that this problem only has one solution: C and B go, and A doesn't. If we convert this to bits, the solution is the string 110, where A is the least significant bit:

```python
# Create an oracle using a Boolean expression
from qiskit.circuit.library import PhaseOracle
oracle = PhaseOracle(
        '(A | B)'    # A must go if B doesn't
        '& ~(A & B & C)' # Can't all go
        '& (B & C)'  # C wants to go with B
        )
```

Figure 7-2 shows the result of `oracle.draw()`. The PhaseOracle constructor has compiled this to a simple diagonal gate that adds a phase of -1 to the state 110. More difficult problems can still be compiled to oracles in polynomial time but won't be as easy to solve by inspection.

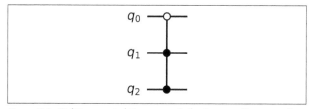

Figure 7-2. Qiskit-generated Grover oracle for the preceding example problem

In the following code snippet, we create an Amplification Problem from our PhaseOracle. Conveniently, the PhaseOracle class has an `evaluate_bitstring` method, which Amplification Problem knows to use as the `is_good_state` parameter, so we don't need to specify that:

```
from qiskit.algorithms import AmplificationProblem
problem = AmplificationProblem(oracle)
```

By default, the AmplificationProblem class defaults to Grover's specific case, but we can set parameters to program other cases:

- The `state_preparation` argument takes a quantum circuit that prepares the state $|A\rangle$. If not specified, this defaults to an H gate on each qubit.

- The `grover_operator` argument takes the circuit that performs $A_\theta B_\theta$. If not specified, Qiskit constructs this from the oracle and `state_preparation` circuit.

- The `post_processing` argument takes a callable Python function that Qiskit will apply to the top measured bit string before writing to the assignment (note this function is not called before passing bit strings to `is_good_state`).

- The `objective_qubits` argument takes a list of integers, which specifies the indexes of the qubits that contain the solution bit string. This is useful if your oracle uses auxiliary qubits that the diffuser and measurements should ignore.

Now that we have our family dynamic problem encoded properly, we can then use Grover's algorithm to solve it. As with all algorithms, we first need to choose the backend to use. In the following code snippet, we use the `AerSimulator`. Once we've constructed the `Grover` object, we can use it to solve the `AmplificationProblem` using the `amplify()` method, which returns a `GroverResult` object. From this `GroverResult` object, we can get the output bit string (plus any postprocessing) via the `assignment` attribute.

Note that since we're happy with the default settings, we can skip creating a `QuantumInstance` and pass our backend straight to `Grover`, which will create this for us:

```
# Choose backend to use
from qiskit.providers.aer import AerSimulator
aer_sim = AerSimulator()

# Use Grover's algorithm to solve the oracle
from qiskit.algorithms import Grover
grover = Grover(quantum_instance=aer_sim)
result = grover.amplify(problem)
result.assignment  # Has value '110'
```

In the preceding code snippet, the algorithm decided the most likely solution was 110, as we expected. Depending on the backend used, we can also access data such as the following:

`circuit_results`
    The raw, unprocessed results of the circuit execution (can be a `Counts` dictionary or `Statevector`).

`top_measurement`
    The most frequently measured bit string.

`max_probability`
> The probability of measuring the most probable bit string.

`iterations`
> Since we might not know how many solutions there are beforehand, the algorithm tries out different powers of Grover iterations, checking the results using the `is_good_state` function. This value is a list of all the powers tried.

Figure 7-3 shows the Grover operator that Qiskit generates from `oracle`. You can access this via `problem.grover_operator`.

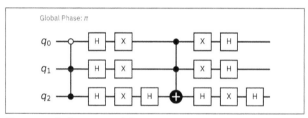

Figure 7-3. Qiskit-generated Grover operator

Phase Estimation Algorithms

Say we have a unitary circuit, Q, and a quantum state, $|\psi\rangle$, and we're guaranteed that $|\psi\rangle$ is an eigenstate of Q, i.e.:

$$Q|\psi\rangle = e^{2\pi i\theta}|\psi\rangle$$

The phase estimation problem is to work out the value of θ.

Qiskit provides three different phase estimation algorithms: `PhaseEstimation`, `HamiltonianPhaseEstimation`, and `Iterative PhaseEstimation`.

`PhaseEstimation` is the classic textbook phase estimation algorithm. It uses two registers, one for the state $|\psi\rangle$ and another "evaluation" register to record the phase Q introduces. The more evaluation qubits, the higher the precision of the output (and the longer the circuit). The algorithm then uses the inverse quantum Fourier transform to read the evaluation register in the computational basis. Figure 7-4 shows an example of this algorithm estimating the phase the T gate introduces to the state $|1\rangle$.

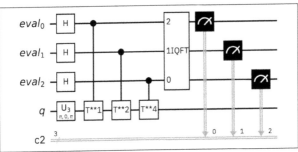

Figure 7-4. A simple phase estimation circuit that estimates the phase the T gate introduces onto the state 1

Each of Qiskit's phase estimation algorithms has an `estimate()` method, which takes a unitary circuit (or other operator) and a circuit that prepares an initial state. The following code shows a simple example for the T gate and the state $|1\rangle$:

```
from qiskit.algorithms import PhaseEstimation
from qiskit.test.mock import FakeSantiago
from qiskit import QuantumCircuit
santiago = FakeSantiago()

# We will first define the problem:
# Our unitary (Q) will be the T gate
unitary = QuantumCircuit(1)
unitary.t(0)

# Our state (|psi>) will be |1>
state_prep = QuantumCircuit(1)
state_prep.x(0)

# Construct our algorithm instance. We will use
# a simulated Santiago device, and three
# evaluation qubits
phase_estimator = PhaseEstimation(3, santiago)
```

```
# Next, run this algorithm on our input problem
result = phase_estimator.estimate(unitary,
                                    state_prep)

# Finally, access the result
result.phase  # Has value: 0.125
```

The `estimate()` method returns a `PhaseEstimationResult`
object, which uses the circuit measurements to guess the most
likely phase and returns a `float`. As with the other algorithms'
Result objects, we can access more than just the most likely
answer. The `PhaseEstimationResult` class has these attributes
and methods:

- The `circuit_result` attribute contains the `Result` object
  from the job run on the backend.

- The `phases` attribute contains a dictionary where the keys
  are measured bit strings and the values are the probability
  of measuring those bit strings.

- The `filter_phases()` method returns the result of the
  phases attribute but with the keys converted from raw bit
  strings to decimal phases.

`HamiltonianPhaseEstimation` is essentially a wrapper for the
`PhaseEstimation` class we explored previously. Instead of a
unitary circuit, `HamiltonianPhaseEstimation.estimate()` takes
a Hermitian operator (as well as a state preparation circuit).
The algorithm then scales and exponentiates the operator,
then runs `PhaseEstimation` on it. `HamiltonianPhaseEstimation`
`.estimate()` has some other optional parameters:

evolution

 A convertor to transform the Hermitian operator to a
 unitary matrix. If unset, then the algorithm uses `Pauli`
 `TrotterEvolution`.

bound

This value limits the magnitude of the operator's eigenvalues, with tighter bounds resulting in better result precision.

IterativePhaseEstimation

This algorithm is the same as `PhaseEstimation`, but instead uses multiple circuits to reduce the evaluation register to just one qubit. You can use the constructor in the same way as the `PhaseEstimation` class. Here, the integer determines the number of iterations, instead of the number of evaluation qubits, but the end result is that both ultimately determine the precision of the output phase.

Amplitude Estimation Algorithms

The *amplitude estimation* problem is very similar to amplitude amplification, but instead of trying to map one state to another, the amplitude estimation problem asks what the inner product of those two states is. For example, given an operator that prepares the state $|a\rangle$ and an operator that rotates around $|b\rangle$, find the value of $\langle a | b \rangle$.

Also like Grover's algorithm, we can easily create an *amplitude estimation* problem from a *counting problem*: given a Boolean function, f, that takes an n-bit string as input and returns a single bit as output, the counting problem asks us for the *number* of bit strings for which f will output 1. For this special case of amplitude estimation, the state $|a\rangle$ is the superposition of all computational basis states, and we can create the operator that rotates around $|b\rangle$ from f using phase kickback.

The `EstimationProblem` class defines an amplitude estimation problem. The only positional arguments are the state preparation circuit (`state_preparation`) and a list of the qubits to operate on (`objective_qubits`). We should also provide a `grover_operator` for our algorithm to perform phase estimation on. Figure 7-5 shows an example of a circuit that performs phase estimation on a Grover operator, Q.

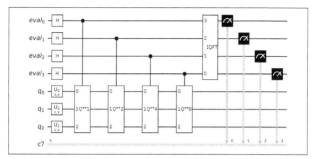

Figure 7-5. Example of a circuit for amplitude estimation, with the Q gate as the Grover operator

In the following code snippet, we'll create an Estimation Problem from a Boolean expression we created in "Grover's Algorithm" on page 124:

```
from qiskit import QuantumCircuit
from qiskit.circuit.library import (PhaseOracle,
                                    GroverOperator)
from qiskit.algorithms import EstimationProblem
oracle = PhaseOracle('(A | B) & ~(A & B & C)'
                     '& (B & C)')

grover_op = GroverOperator(oracle)

# Create state preparation operator
n = oracle.num_qubits
state_prep = QuantumCircuit(n)
state_prep.h(range(n))

problem = EstimationProblem(state_prep,
                            [*range(n)],
                        grover_operator=grover_op)
```

Now that we've defined our problem, let's use an algorithm to solve it. First, we'll use Qiskit's AmplitudeEstimation algorithm. This is the original amplitude estimation algorithm that performs phase estimation on a Grover operator. In the following code snippet, we create an `AmplitudeEstimation` instance with nine counting qubits.

We happen to know already that this problem uses three bits (and so `oracle.num_qubits == 3`) and has one solution, so we expect the result to be $1/2^3 = 0.125$:

```
from qiskit.algorithms import AmplitudeEstimation
from qiskit.providers.aer import AerSimulator
aer_sim = AerSimulator()

# Create algorithm with nine counting qubits
estimator = AmplitudeEstimation(9,
                                quantum_instance=aer_sim)
result = estimator.estimate(problem)
result.estimation  # Has value: 0.1254318
```

We can see that the value of `result.estimation` is what we expected.

Eigensolvers

An *eigensolver* is an algorithm that finds the eigenvalues (and/or eigenvectors) of a matrix. Since classical computers can solve eigenvalue problems in time polynomial with the size of the input matrix, the difficulty is when we want to solve polynomial sums of Pauli operators that result in exponentially large matrices.

For example, let's use Qiskit's `opflow` module to create a simple operator:

```
from qiskit.opflow import X, Y, Z, I

op = ( .5 * (X ^ Y ^ Z)
     + .2 * (Y ^ Y ^ I)
     - .3 * (Z ^ X ^ Z)
     + .2 * (I ^ X ^ Y))
op.to_matrix().size  # Has value 64
```

We can see that the size of this operator's matrix is much larger than the number of operator terms.

When most of the traditional quantum algorithms were developed, quantum computers were nonexistent, and we didn't even know what they would look like. The only concern was asymptotic scaling; the specific gate count was unimportant. These early pioneers showed that investing in quantum computing would be worth the effort *eventually*, but now that we have small, working devices, another important question is "What can we do that might be useful *soon*?"

Qiskit implements a few near-term algorithms (algorithms with small numbers of qubits and lower gate fidelities in mind). At the time of writing, these are all types of minimum eigensolvers; i.e., eigensolvers that find only the smallest eigenvalue.

NumPy Eigensolvers

At the time of writing, Qiskit provides only one algorithm to find all eigenvalues of an operator: the classical NumPyEigen solver. This code shows how to use the NumPyEigensolver to find all the eigenvalues of op:

```
from qiskit.algorithms import NumPyEigensolver
np_solver = NumPyEigensolver(k=10)
result = np_solver.compute_eigenvalues(op)
print(result.eigenvalues.real)
```

Which prints the output:

```
[-0.89442719 -0.89442719 -0.2        -0.2
  0.2         0.2         0.89442719  0.89442719]
```

As with all algorithms, we start by creating an instance of the algorithm through the NumPyEigensolver constructor. This constructor takes two optional arguments:

k

The number of eigenvalues to compute. This is 1 by default, which is also the minimum value (otherwise it wouldn't need to compute anything). In the preceding example, we set this to 10, which is higher than the dimension of the matrix, so we got all eight eigenvalues.

filter_criterion
> This is a callable object that takes three parameters: an eigenstate, that state's eigenvalue, and a tuple containing the mean and standard deviation (called aux_values). It returns True if we want to keep this eigenstate/value, or False to ignore it.

We can then use the compute_eigenvalues method to execute the algorithm, giving the operator as a positional parameter. This method returns an EigensolverResult object, which has three attributes:

- eigenvalues
- eigenstates
- aux_operator_eigenvalues (tuples of the mean and standard deviations for each eigenvalue, for algorithms with some uncertainty)

The following code shows a different instance of the NumPy Eigensolver with different constructor arguments applied to the preceding problem:

```
def ignore_negative(state, value, aux):
    return value >= 0   # bool

np_solver = NumPyEigensolver(k=3,
                filter_criterion=ignore_negative)
result = np_solver.compute_eigenvalues(op)
result.eigenvalues.real   # [0.2, 0.2, 0.89442719]
```

Some quantum systems (e.g., molecules) are very difficult to simulate with classical computers (i.e., we don't have polynomial-time classical algorithms for simulating them). Despite this, we still find these systems in nature, so they must be solvable at least by a universal quantum computer. This quantum simulation problem was one of the earliest proposed applications of programmable quantum computers and is believed to be one of the more realistic near-term applications of quantum computing.

The problem of quantum simulation boils down to solving the Schrödinger equation for a specific Hamiltonian, which is a description of how the quantum system evolves with time. The eigenvalues of a Hamiltonian are the possible energies the system can have. We can convert a Hamiltonian into a matrix (which must be Hermitian, as the energy is a real number) and then use an eigensolver to find the allowed energies of the system. If we can write a Hamiltonian as a polynomially sized sum of Pauli operators, then we can simulate this Hamiltonian efficiently on our quantum computer but not necessarily on a classical computer.

Since systems are usually more stable at their lower energy levels, the lowest possible energy of a system is often the most interesting. Qiskit's quantum eigensolvers are all minimum eigensolvers that aim to find only this smallest energy eigenvalue.

The next algorithm we will look at is the `NumPyMinimumEigen` solver, which is the same algorithm as the `NumPyEigensolver` but returns only the lowest eigenvalue/vector. We can use this algorithm to check the accuracy of our quantum algorithms for relatively small matrices:

```
from qiskit.algorithms import (
                NumPyMinimumEigensolver)
np_min_solver = NumPyMinimumEigensolver()
result = np_min_solver.compute_minimum_eigenvalue(
                                            op)
```

As with the `NumPyEigensolver`, we can also provide an optional `filter_criterion` function to ignore certain eigenvalues/states. The returned result object also has `eigenstate` and `aux_opera tor_eigenvalues` attributes.

The Variational Quantum Eigensolver

Next, we'll look at the famous variational quantum eigensolver. This algorithm uses the fact that quantum computers can perform Hamiltonians efficiently, and uses this to calculate the expectation value of the Hamiltonian. The lowest possible expectation value we can measure will be the lowest eigenvalue of the Hamiltonian (when the state is its corresponding eigenstate).

The variational algorithms use a parameterized quantum circuit to prepare different quantum states. The algorithm measures the expectation values of these states, then uses a classical optimizer to try to find the lowest expectation value (that will hopefully also be the lowest eigenvalue).

We can create an instance of this algorithm using the VQE class. The constructor has two required arguments: the parameterized circuit and the backend we'll run the algorithm on. For this simple example, we'll use EfficientSU2 from the circuit library and the AerSimulator's statevector method:

```
from qiskit.providers.aer import AerSimulator
from qiskit.algorithms import VQE
from qiskit.circuit.library import EfficientSU2

circuit = EfficientSU2()
vqe = VQE(circuit,
          quantum_instance=AerSimulator(
                     method='statevector')
          )
result = vqe.compute_minimum_eigenvalue(op)
result.eigenvalue.real  # -0.8944268580187336
```

The compute_minimum_eigenvalue method returns a result object with an eigenvalue attribute. Comparing this with the NumPyMinimumEigensolver result, we can see the algorithm has found the correct minimum eigenvalue. The MinimumEigen solverResult object returned by the Variational Quantum Eigensolver (VQE) algorithm also has some other attributes, including the following:

```
result.cost_function_evals  # Has value: 477
```

This result shows the number of times the algorithm measured the expectation value of the operator. The result object also contains the circuit parameters that create this best eigenstate (optimal_parameters, or optimal_point, depending on if you want a dictionary or a list) and the time taken by the algorithm (optimizer_time).

The VQE constructor also takes other optional arguments. One useful argument is the callback argument, which lets us call custom code at each step of the optimization. This argument takes a callable that has four positional arguments:

Evaluation count
    The number of steps taken so far in the optimization.

Parameters
    The parameters of the parameterized circuit at this point in the optimization. If everything's going well, this will usually be the best-known parameters so far.

Mean
    This is the estimated expectation value at this point in the optimization.

Standard deviation
    The standard deviation of the distribution averaged to find the mean.

The following code creates a simple class with a method that accepts these values and stores some of them for analysis afterward. You might also use a callback to print updates throughout the optimization:

```python
class VQELog():
    def __init__(self):
        self.counts = []
        self.params = []
        self.means = []
    def callback(self, eval_count, params,
                             mean, std_dev):
        self.counts.append(eval_count)
        self.params.append(params)
        self.means.append(mean)
```

In the following code, we run VQE again with the callback and use this info to draw a graph showing how the algorithm progresses with each step:

```
log = VQELog()
vqe = VQE(circuit,
          callback=log.callback,
          quantum_instance=AerSimulator(
                      method='statevector')
          )
result = vqe.compute_minimum_eigenvalue(op)
result.eigenvalue.real  # -0.8944268580187336

import matplotlib.pyplot as plt
plt.plot(log.counts, log.means);
```

Figure 7-6 shows the plot created by the preceding code.

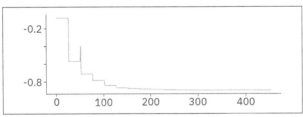

Figure 7-6. Graph of mean versus evaluation count

Another useful argument is the initial_point argument. By default, the VQE algorithm chooses a random set of numbers as starting circuit parameters, but if we have a good idea where the minimum might be, this argument allows us to start the algorithm from that point instead. For example, let's start our algorithm off closer to the minimum; the preceding code runs the VQE algorithm as before but starting with the parameters the algorithm discovered in the 200th optimization step in the preceding results:

```
initial_point = log.params[200]
log = VQELog()
vqe = VQE(circuit,
          callback=log.callback,
```

```
                 initial_point=initial_point,
                 quantum_instance=AerSimulator(
                              method='statevector')
        )
result = vqe.compute_minimum_eigenvalue(op)
result.eigenvalue.real  # -0.8944270665137739
plt.plot(log.counts, log.means);
```

Figure 7-7 shows the plot created by the preceding code.

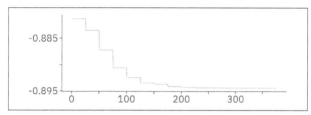

Figure 7-7. Graph of mean versus evaluation count for an algorithm starting at a point close to the optimal point

We can see that the algorithm found the minimum much faster.

Parameterized Circuits

We can also adjust the VQE algorithm by choosing a different form of parameterized circuit. In the previous section, we used the EfficientSU2 circuit from Qiskit's library, but we could also use other circuits, depending on the application. For example, the TwoLocal circuit has fewer parameters, and so can converge much faster, but has the downside of not being able to create as many quantum states:

```
from qiskit.circuit.library import (EfficientSU2,
                                     TwoLocal)
len(EfficientSU2(3).parameters)  # 24
len(TwoLocal(3, 'ry', 'cx').parameters)  # 12
```

In the following code cell, we use the TwoLocal circuit, with layers of RY and CX gates. The algorithm performs poorly and converges on a value close to -0.5 because this version of the TwoLocal gate can't create the lowest eigenstate of the operator:

```
log = VQELog()
vqe = VQE(TwoLocal(3, 'ry', 'cx'),
          callback=log.callback,
          quantum_instance=AerSimulator(
                    method='statevector')
          )
result = vqe.compute_minimum_eigenvalue(op)
plt.plot(log.counts, log.means);
result.eigenvalue.real  # -0.49999960316294956
```

Figure 7-8 shows the plot created by the preceding code.

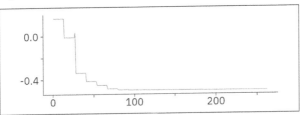

Figure 7-8. Graph of mean versus evaluation count for an algorithm using a poor parameterized circuit

If instead we use layers of rx and cx gates, we get much closer. The result is still not as close as with the EfficientSU2 circuit, but this circuit converges much faster and gets within 1% of the correct value:

```
log = VQELog()
vqe = VQE(TwoLocal(3, 'rx', 'cx'),
          callback=log.callback,
          quantum_instance=AerSimulator(
                    method='statevector')
          )
result = vqe.compute_minimum_eigenvalue(op)
result.eigenvalue.real  # -0.8890712131577212
plt.plot(log.counts, log.means);
```

Figure 7-9 shows the plot created by the preceding code.

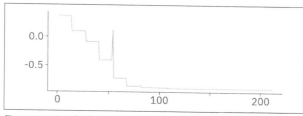

Figure 7-9. Graph of mean versus evaluation count for an algorithm using a good parameterized circuit

We can use any parameterized circuit with VQE, but some are more useful than others. We generally prefer circuits that can create many states (better chance it can create our specific eigenstate) but that also scale efficiently enough to be useful on near-term devices. Qiskit's circuit library contains some circuits designed for this use, known as *N-local* circuits.

Qiskit's N-local circuits have two layers: a *rotation* layer and an *entangling* layer. The rotation layer is a set of gates that act only on single qubits, or on small subsets of qubits. The entangling layer is usually where the parameters are. This is a set of multiqubit (e.g., CCX) gates aimed to help us create entangled states.

The most general of these is the NLocal circuit. In the following code snippet, we create an NLocal circuit with three qubits, using YGates in the rotation layers and CZGates in the entangling layers:

```python
from qiskit.circuit.library import NLocal
from qiskit.circuit.library import RYGate, CZGate
from qiskit.circuit import Parameter
NLocal(3, # Number of qubits
       # Gate in rotation layer
       RYGate(Parameter('theta')),
       # Gates in entangling layer
       CZGate(),
       # Entangling gate pattern
       reps=3)
```

Figure 7-10 shows the circuit created in the preceding code snippet, decomposed one layer.

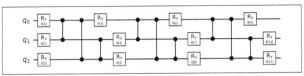

Figure 7-10. Example of an N-local circuit

With `entanglement='full'`, the entangling layers perform gates between each possible qubit pair, but the number of gates this introduces scales quadratically with the number of qubits. We can instead change this to `'linear'`, `'circular'`, or `'sca'` for different entangling schemes that each use around one entangling gate per qubit. We can also choose how many times the circuit repeats through the `reps` argument, which is 1 by default.

A specific case of the `NLocal` circuit is the `TwoLocal` circuit, which we've already seen in action as a parameterized circuit. This circuit template has layers of single-qubit gates, followed by layers of two-qubit entangling gates (e.g., CNOTs). As we saw earlier, we can choose the gates this circuit uses in the rotation layers using strings, but we could also pass `Gate` or `QuantumCircuit` objects instead. Here, `reps` is 3 by default, so the following line:

```
from qiskit.circuit.library import TwoLocal
TwoLocal(3, 'ry', 'cz')
```

creates the same circuit as the `NLocal` circuit we created previously (shown decomposed in Figure 7-10).

Another example is the `RealAmplitudes` circuit, a special case of `TwoLocal`, in which the single-qubit gates are RY gates and the two-qubit gates are CX gates. This circuit produces states with only real amplitudes (i.e., phase = 0), hence the name.

Optimizers

The other key factor in variational algorithms is the classical program that decides how to twiddle the parameters to minimize or maximize the expectation value. Qiskit calls these programs *optimizers* and stores them under `qiskit.algorithms.optimizers`. In this guide, we will focus on *local* optimizers, which aim to find only local extrema and not necessarily the absolute lowest- or highest-possible energy. At the time of writing, Qiskit provides roughly 20 local optimizers.

Figure 7-11 shows a few different local optimizers finding the minimum of a very simple landscape, with only two parameters. The x- and y-axes are the different possible values of the parameters, and the height of the surface shows the expectation value for those parameters. The black lines show the path the optimizers took, and the dots show the different "points" at each step in the optimization process. Note that performance on this landscape with these arguments might not be indicative of performance in general.

At a high level, each of these optimizers evaluates the expectation value for a set of parameters (which we'll call a *point*), and then uses this information to guess which new points might have better expectation values. As we saw previously, we can specify a starting point if we have a good idea of where the optimal value might be, or VQE can choose a random starting point for us.

For example, `GradientDescent` is a simple algorithm that estimates the gradient at its current point by measuring the difference in expectation values for small changes (perturbations) in the parameters. The algorithm then moves a step in the direction of steepest downward descent.

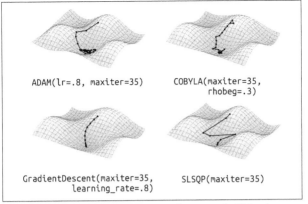

Figure 7-11. How different optimizers explore a simple 2D landscape

We can tell the VQE algorithm to use this optimizer through the `optimizer` parameter in the following code snippet. We'll try this out with the default parameters:

```
from qiskit.algorithms.optimizers import (
                                GradientDescent)
log = VQELog()
vqe = VQE(EfficientSU2(),
          optimizer=GradientDescent(),
          callback=log.callback,
          quantum_instance=AerSimulator(
                      method='statevector')
          )
result = vqe.compute_minimum_eigenvalue(op)
result.eigenvalue.real  # -0.5997810307109372
```

The algorithm performed pretty poorly here. We know this parameterized circuit can achieve the correct value of ~ -0.894, so what happened? If we look at the log (Figure 7-12), we can see the algorithm used 2,500 evaluations (the default maximum for GradientDescent), so the optimizer timed out before reaching the best value.

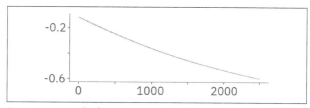

Figure 7-12. Graph of mean versus evaluation count for each point in the VQE search using gradient descent

We can see the optimizer was heading toward the minimum correctly, but the steps were too small to get there in time. We could increase the number of iterations through the Gradient Descent's 'maxiter' parameter, or better yet, change the size of steps through the 'learning_rate' parameter. The default is 0.01, so in the following code snippet, we set it to 0.2 to speed up convergence:

```
log = VQELog()
vqe = VQE(EfficientSU2(),
          optimizer=GradientDescent(
              learning_rate=0.2
              ),
          callback=log.callback,
          quantum_instance=AerSimulator(
                      method='statevector')
          )
result = vqe.compute_minimum_eigenvalue(op)
result.eigenvalue.real  # -0.8938653211271332
```

Figure 7-13 shows how the GradientDescent algorithm converges as it progresses. The optimizer approaches the value faster but still hits the maximum evaluation count before converging.

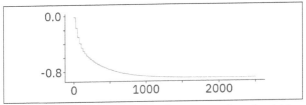

Figure 7-13. Graph of mean versus evaluation count for each point in the VQE search using gradient descent, with a larger learning rate

This performs much better but still doesn't converge before running out of evaluations.

For better performance, we can instead use the COBYLA algorithm (Constrained Optimization By Linear Approximation, also known as Powell's method). This method doesn't need to estimate the gradient at each point, which saves circuit runs. Instead, the algorithm roughly calculates the gradient with a couple of evaluations (seen in the triangle-like path at the start of the optimization in Figure 7-11), then optimizes along a 1D line. Once it hits that constrained minimum, it chooses a new direction based on the approximated gradient and does another constrained optimization along this new line:

```
from qiskit.algorithms.optimizers import COBYLA
log = VQELog()
vqe = VQE(EfficientSU2(),
          optimizer=COBYLA(),
          callback=log.callback,
          quantum_instance=AerSimulator(
                      method='statevector')
          )
result = vqe.compute_minimum_eigenvalue(op)
result.eigenvalue.real  # -0.8944270576823009
```

Figure 7-14 plots the measured expectation values for each evaluation from the preceding code.

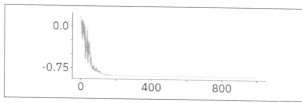

Figure 7-14. Graph of expectation value versus evaluation count for each point in the VQE search using COBYLA

This short example shows that the choice of optimizer can make a big difference in the performance of our algorithms. Qiskit provides many optimizers, each with different arguments, behaviors, and performance levels on different tasks.

PART III
Additional Essential Functionality

You know the Wolfman's just about the
number one cat alive

—Todd Rundgren

In Part I we discussed fundamentals of quantum computing with Qiskit, and in Part II we demonstrated features of Qiskit that leverage the power of quantum information. Here in Part III, we'll discuss various modules and features of Qiskit that are also essential for quantum application developers. First, Chapter 8, "Qiskit Circuit Library Standard Operations" serves as a reference for gates and instructions introduced in Part I.

Chapter 9, "Working with Providers and Backends" demonstrates features of Qiskit that abstract and facilitate working with various quantum computers and simulators.

Finally, we'll explore the quantum assembly language QASM 3.0 in Chapter 10, "OpenQASM".

Qiskit Circuit Library Standard Operations

The Qiskit Circuit Library (module `qiskit.circuit.library`) contains many operations and circuits that may be used as building blocks for implementing quantum algorithms. Here are some standard operations categorized as instructions, single-qubit gates, and multiqubit gates.

Standard Instructions

The standard instruction classes implement quantum operations that aren't necessarily unitary. They are subclasses of the `Instruction` class (see "The Instruction Class" on page 26).

Barrier

The `Barrier` class creates a barrier instruction (see "Creating a barrier" on page 10) with a given number of qubits. A barrier provides both visual and functional separation between gates on a wire in a quantum circuit:

Signature	Appearance
Barrier(num_qubits)	

Measure

The Measure class creates a measurement instruction for measuring a quantum state in the computational basis, placing the binary result in a classical register (see "Measuring a quantum circuit" on page 11):

Signature	Appearance
Measure()	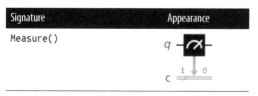

Reset

The Reset class creates a reset instruction that resets the qubit state to $|0\rangle$ (see "Using the reset() method" on page 19):

Signature	Appearance
Reset()	$q - |0\rangle -$

Standard Single-Qubit Gates

The standard single-qubit gates implement unitary quantum operations. They are subclasses of the Gate class (see "The Gate Class" on page 27). These gates may be created and applied to a circuit via the single-qubit gate methods of the QuantumCircuit class that appear in Table 1-1.

HGate

The HGate class creates a single-qubit H gate. It performs a π rotation around the X + Z axis. It also has the effect of changing the computational basis from $|0\rangle, |1\rangle$ to $|+\rangle, |-\rangle$ and vice-versa:

Signature	Appearance	Matrix
HGate(label=None)	$q - H -$	$\frac{1}{\sqrt{2}}\begin{pmatrix} 1 & 1 \\ 1 & -1 \end{pmatrix}$

IGate

The IGate class creates a single-qubit I gate, which has no effect on the state of a qubit:

Signature	Appearance	Matrix
IGate(label=None)	$q - I -$	$\begin{pmatrix} 1 & 0 \\ 0 & 1 \end{pmatrix}$

PhaseGate

The PhaseGate class creates a single-qubit Phase gate that performs a given phase rotation:

Signature	Appearance	Matrix
PhaseGate(theta, label=None)	$q - P_{\pi/2} -$	$\begin{pmatrix} 1 & 0 \\ 0 & e^{i\lambda} \end{pmatrix}$

RXGate

The RXGate class creates a single-qubit RX gate that performs a given rotation around the X-axis:

Signature	Appearance	Matrix
RXGate(theta, label=None)	$q - \boxed{R_X}_{\pi/2} -$	$\begin{pmatrix} \cos\frac{\theta}{2} & -i\sin\frac{\theta}{2} \\ -i\sin\frac{\theta}{2} & \cos\frac{\theta}{2} \end{pmatrix}$

RYGate

The RYGate class creates a single-qubit RY gate that performs a given rotation around the Y-axis:

Signature	Appearance	Matrix
RYGate(theta, label=None)	$q - \boxed{R_Y}_{\pi/2} -$	$\begin{pmatrix} \cos\frac{\theta}{2} & -\sin\frac{\theta}{2} \\ \sin\frac{\theta}{2} & \cos\frac{\theta}{2} \end{pmatrix}$

RZGate

The RZGate class creates a single-qubit RZ gate that performs a given rotation around the Z-axis:

Signature	Appearance	Matrix
RZGate(phi, label=None)	$q - \boxed{R_Z}_{\pi/2} -$	$\begin{pmatrix} e^{-i\frac{\lambda}{2}} & 0 \\ 0 & e^{i\frac{\lambda}{2}} \end{pmatrix}$

SGate

The SGate class creates a single-qubit S gate that performs a $\pi/2$ phase rotation:

Signature	Appearance	Matrix
SGate(label=None)	$q - \boxed{S} -$	$\begin{pmatrix} 1 & 0 \\ 0 & i \end{pmatrix}$

SdgGate

The SdgGate class creates a single-qubit $S^\dagger$ gate that performs a $-\pi/2$ phase rotation:

Signature	Appearance	Matrix
SdgGate(label=None)	$q - S^\dagger -$	$\begin{pmatrix} 1 & 0 \\ 0 & -i \end{pmatrix}$

SXGate

The SXGate class creates a single-qubit square root of X gate that performs a $\pi/2$ rotation around the X-axis while shifting the global phase by $\pi/4$:

Signature	Appearance	Matrix
SXGate(label=None)	$q - \sqrt{X} -$	$\frac{1}{2}\begin{pmatrix} 1+i & 1-i \\ 1-i & 1+i \end{pmatrix}$

SXdgGate

The SXdgGate class creates a single-qubit inverse square root of X gate that performs a $-\pi/2$ rotation around the X-axis while shifting the global phase by $-\pi/4$:

Signature	Appearance	Matrix
SXdgGate(label=None)	$q - \sqrt{X}^\dagger -$	$\frac{1}{2}\begin{pmatrix} 1-i & 1+i \\ 1+i & 1-i \end{pmatrix}$

TGate

The TGate class creates a single-qubit T gate that performs a $\pi/4$ phase rotation:

Signature	Appearance	Matrix
TGate(label=None)	$q - T -$	$\begin{pmatrix} 1 & 0 \\ 0 & e^{j\pi/4} \end{pmatrix}$

TdgGate

The TdgGate class creates a single-qubit $T^\dagger$ gate that performs a $-\pi/4$ phase rotation:

Signature	Appearance	Matrix
TdgGate(label=None)	$q - \boxed{T^\dagger} -$	$\begin{pmatrix} 1 & 0 \\ 0 & e^{-i\pi/4} \end{pmatrix}$

UGate

The UGate class creates a single-qubit U gate with three Euler angles:

Signature	Appearance	Matrix
UGate(theta, phi, lam, label=None)	$q - \boxed{\begin{smallmatrix}U\\\pi/2,0,\pi\end{smallmatrix}} -$	$\begin{pmatrix} \cos(\flat) & -e^{j\lambda}\sin(\flat) \\ e^{j\varphi}\sin(\flat) & e^{j(\varphi+\lambda)}\cos(\flat) \end{pmatrix}$

XGate

The XGate class creates a single-qubit X gate that performs a π rotation around the X-axis:

Signature	Appearance	Matrix
XGate(label=None)	$q - \boxed{X} -$	$\begin{pmatrix} 0 & 1 \\ 1 & 0 \end{pmatrix}$

YGate

The YGate class creates a single-qubit Y gate that performs a π rotation around the Y-axis:

Signature	Appearance	Matrix
YGate(label=None)	$q - \boxed{Y} -$	$\begin{pmatrix} 0 & -i \\ i & 0 \end{pmatrix}$

ZGate

The ZGate class creates a single-qubit Z gate that performs a π rotation around the Z-axis:

Signature	Appearance	Matrix
ZGate(label=None)	$q - \boxed{Z} -$	$\begin{pmatrix} 1 & 0 \\ 0 & -1 \end{pmatrix}$

Standard Multiqubit Gates

The standard multiqubit gates implement unitary quantum operations. They are subclasses of the ControlledGate class (see "The ControlledGate Class" on page 29). Some of these gates may be created and applied to a circuit via the multiqubit gate methods of the QuantumCircuit class, many of which appear in Table 1-2.

C3XGate

The C3XGate class creates a four-qubit gate that has an X gate and three control qubits:

Signature	Appearance
C3XGate(label=None, ctrl_state=None)	

C3SXGate

The C3SXGate class creates a four-qubit gate that has a square root of X gate and three control qubits:

Signature	Appearance
C3SXGate(label=None, ctrl_state=None, *, angle=None)	q_0 ——●—— q_1 ——●—— q_2 ——●—— q_3 —$\sqrt{X}$—

C4XGate

The C4XGate class creates a five-qubit gate that has an X gate and four control qubits:

Signature	Appearance
C4XGate(label=None, ctrl_state=None)	q_0 ——●—— q_1 ——●—— q_2 ——●—— q_3 ——●—— q_4 ——⊕——

CCXGate

The CCXGate class creates a three-qubit gate that has an X gate and two control qubits. This is also known as a Toffoli gate:

Signature	Appearance
CCXGate(label=None, ctrl_state=None)	q_0 ——●—— q_1 ——●—— q_2 ——⊕——

CHGate

The CHGate class creates a controlled-Hadamard gate, applying the Hadamard according to the control qubit state:

Signature	Appearance
CHGate(label=None, ctrl_state=None)	q_0 ——•—— q_1 —[H]—

CPhaseGate

The CPhaseGate class creates a controlled-phase gate, applying the PhaseGate according to the control qubit state:

Signature	Appearance
CPhaseGate(theta, label=None, ctrl_state=None)	q_0 ——•—— P (π/2) q_1 ——•——

CRXGate

The CRXGate class creates a controlled-RX gate, applying the RX according to the control qubit state:

Signature	Appearance
CRXGate(theta, label=None, ctrl_state=None)	q_0 ——•—— q_1 —[R_X π/2]—

CRYGate

The CRYGate class creates a controlled-RY gate, applying the RY according to the control qubit state:

Signature	Appearance
CRYGate(theta, label=None, ctrl_state=None)	q_0 ——●—— q_1 — R_Y $\pi/2$ —

CRZGate

The CRZGate class creates a controlled-RZ gate, applying the RZ according to the control qubit state:

Signature	Appearance
CRZGate(theta, label=None, ctrl_state=None)	q_0 ——●—— q_1 — R_Z $\pi/2$ —

CSwapGate

The CSwapGate class creates a three-qubit gate whose Swap gate is applied according to the control qubit state:

Signature	Appearance
CSwapGate(label=None, ctrl_state=None)	q_0 ——●—— q_1 ——✕—— q_2 ——✕——

CSXGate

The CSXGate class creates a controlled-SX (square root of X) gate, applying the $\sqrt{X}$ gate according to the control qubit state:

Signature	Appearance
CSXGate(label=None, ctrl_state=None)	q_0 ——●—— q_1 —$\sqrt{X}$—

CUGate

The CUGate class creates a controlled-U gate, applying the U gate, including a global phase argument, according to the control qubit state:

Signature	Appearance
CUGate(theta, phi, lam, gamma, label=None, ctrl_state=None)	q_0 ——●—— q_1 — U π/2, 0, π, 0

CXGate

The CXGate class creates a controlled-X gate, applying the X gate according to the control qubit state:

Signature	Appearance
CXGate(label=None, ctrl_state=None)	q_0 ——●—— q_1 —⊕—

CYGate

The CYGate class creates a controlled-Y gate, applying the Y gate according to the control qubit state:

Signature	Appearance
CYGate(label=None, ctrl_state=None)	q_0 ——●—— q_1 — Y —

CZGate

The CZGate class creates a controlled-Z gate, applying the Z gate according to the control qubit state:

Signature	Appearance
CZGate(label=None, ctrl_state=None)	q_0 ——●—— ｜ q_1 ——●——

DCXGate

The DCXGate class creates a double-CNOT gate. This is a two-qubit gate that has two CNOT gates with their control-qubits on different wires:

Signature	Appearance
DCXGate()	q_0 ——●——⊕—— q_1 ——⊕——●——

iSwapGate

The iSwapGate class swaps the qubit states of two quantum wires. It also changes the phase of $|01\rangle$ and $|10\rangle$ amplitudes by i:

Signature	Appearance
iSwapGate(label=None, ctrl_state=None)	q_0 —⎡ 0 ⎤— ⎢ Iswap ⎥ q_1 —⎣ 1 ⎦—

MCPhaseGate

The MCPhaseGate class creates a multicontrolled phase gate with a given number of control qubits:

Signature	Appearance
MCPhaseGate(lam, num_ctrl_qubits, label=None)	

MCXGate

The MCXGate class creates a multicontrolled X gate with a given number of control qubits. This is a generalization of a Toffoli gate:

Signature	Appearance
MCXGate(num_ctrl_qubits=None , label=None, ctrl_state=None)	

SwapGate

The SwapGate swaps the qubit states of two quantum wires:

Signature	Appearance
SwapGate(label=None)	

## CHAPTER 9

Working with Providers and Backends

There are lots of different ways to run quantum circuits and quantum algorithms. If we want to see how a noise-free quantum computer behaves, we could choose from a few different simulators (e.g., statevector or unitary), and we're not limited to just local simulators. Chances are, at some point you will want to run a circuit on a real quantum system, accessed remotely.

To manage all these options, and ensure all backends are compatible with the same data types, Qiskit defines a general Backend object. This makes it easier to interchange backends in our code (and also to remember what the right code is in the first place). You've already seen these Backend objects in action, as we use the Backend.run() method every time we run a circuit. Real quantum systems have unique properties that can change regularly. The Backend object also helps us access this information so we can investigate different systems and make decisions about which systems to use. We can access this information both programmatically and through graphical user interfaces.

These Backend objects are organized by *providers*. If you've read the rest of this book, you will have used the Aer and

`BasicAer` providers, which manage simulator backends that run on your local machine (e.g., using `.get_backend()` to retrieve a backend object by name), but we can install other providers to use other backends (real or simulated). Examples are the IBM Quantum provider (from the `qiskit-ibmq-provider` Python package) through which we can access IBM Quantum's online backends or the IonQ provider (from the `qiskit-ionq` package) to access IonQ's online backends.

Qiskit and its provider interface allow us to search through these backends and provide some useful functionality for remote services that we'll explore later in this chapter. In this chapter, we'll use IBM Quantum's provider for the examples, but other providers are available, and you can even write your own. To set up a provider for remote backends, you'll usually need to make an account with them and save an API key to your environment. The code for IBM Quantum is shown here, but other providers will have their own instructions:

```
from qiskit import IBMQ
IBMQ.save_account('API_TOKEN')
```

Qiskit stores your token as an environment variable, so you need to save your account only once. You can then access the open provider using the following code:

```
from qiskit import IBMQ
provider = IBMQ.load_account()
```

Graphical Tools

For users working in Jupyter environments, Qiskit provides some graphical tools. You can install these using the following command:

```
pip install qiskit[visualization]
```

Once installed, we can activate these tools with this line of code:

```
import qiskit.tools.jupyter
```

This will enable some Jupyter "magics" (commands specific to this environment) and will patch some objects to enable richer representations.

We can see this in action here. We import a mock backend and ask Jupyter to display it by returning it as the last line in the cell:

```
from qiskit.test.mock import FakeVigo
FakeVigo()
```

Figure 9-1 shows the output of the preceding code in a Jupyter Notebook:

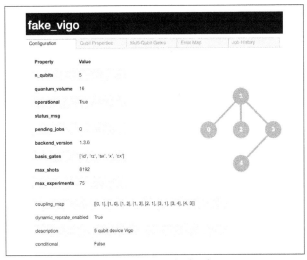

Figure 9-1. Screenshot of the interactive backend GUI in a Jupyter Notebook

This displays an interactive panel with images and switchable tabs. We can also now use magic commands, such as %qiskit_version_table, which displays the Qiskit version information as an HTML table. If we have the IBM Quantum provider set up, we can use the %backend_overview command to display an interface with information on its remote systems (such as queue times and system properties).

Figure 9-2 shows the %backend_overview GUI in a Jupyter Notebook cell.

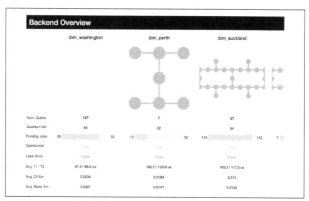

Figure 9-2. The backend overview GUI in a Jupyter Notebook, showing details and status of available backends

Text-Based Tools

For non-Jupyter environments, some tools are also available as text-based tools. For example, there is a Python function with a similar job to the %backend_overview magic:

```
from qiskit.tools import backend_overview
backend_overview()
```

The preceding code prints output similar to the text that follows. The output will depend on the backends available, and some text is omitted to save space:

```
ibm_washington               ibm_perth
--------------               ---------
Num. Qubits:   127           Num. Qubits:   7
Pending Jobs:  133           Pending Jobs:  1
Least busy:    False         Least busy:    False
Operational:   True          Operational:   True
```

```
   Avg. T1:      97.2              Avg. T1:      173.6
   Avg. T2:      96.5              Avg. T2:      133.9


   ibm_cairo                       ibm_lagos
   ---------                       ---------
   Num. Qubits: 27                 Num. Qubits: 7
   Pending Jobs: 7                 Pending Jobs: 9
   Least busy:   False             Least busy:   False
   Operational: True               Operational: True
   Avg. T1:      96.6              Avg. T1:      145.5
   Avg. T2:      107.1             Avg. T2:      109.3
```

Similarly, we can print a textual summary of a backend using the backend_monitor function:

```python
from qiskit import IBMQ
provider = IBMQ.load_account()
armonk = provider.get_backend('ibmq_armonk')

from qiskit.tools import backend_monitor
backend_monitor(armonk)
```

This code will print output similar to the output that follows (again, some text is omitted, and the values will change depending on the backend):

```
ibmq_armonk
===========
Configuration
-------------
    n_qubits: 1
    operational: True
    status_msg: active
    pending_jobs: 80
    backend_version: 2.4.29
    basis_gates: ['id', 'rz', 'sx', 'x']
    local: False
    simulator: False
    conditional_latency: []
    ...
```

Getting System Info Programmatically

We can also get a backend's information in a format that's easy to work with in Python. This is how the transpiler knows how to prepare and optimize a circuit for a specific system, given only the backend object. Qiskit splits information about a backend into three categories:

Configuration
> Information about the system that doesn't change with time. Examples include the number of qubits and the coupling map. We access this through the `.configuration()` method.

Properties
> Information that *can* change with time and requires remeasuring and calibrating. Examples include the gate errors and decoherence times of the qubits. We access this through the `.properties()` method.

Options
> The default settings used when running jobs on the backend. We can override these when using the `.run()` method (e.g., `.run(qc, shots=2048)`) or change these defaults for an instance of a backend. We access these through the `.options` attribute.

We can pair these methods and attributes with the provider interface to automatically select backends that fit certain criteria. The last line in the following code snippet returns a list of backends that are *not* simulators and that have more than three qubits:

```
def is_ok_backend(backend):
    return (
        not backend.configuration().simulator
        and backend.configuration().num_qubits > 3)

provider.backends(filters=is_ok_backend)
```

The data available from `.configuration()` and `.properties()` depends on the backend, but we can inspect this using Python's `vars()` function. In the next code snippet, we show the information available from the `FakeVigo` device (we've omitted some text to save space):

```
from qiskit.test.mock import FakeVigo
vars(FakeVigo().configuration())

{'_data': {'allow_q_object': True,
  'meas_map': [[0, 1, 2, 3, 4]],
  'multi_meas_enabled': False,
  'quantum_volume': 16,
  'url': 'None',
  'allow_object_storage': True},
 'backend_name': 'fake_vigo',
 'backend_version': '1.3.6',
 'n_qubits': 5,
 'basis_gates': ['id', 'rz', 'sx', 'x', 'cx'],
 ...
 'online_date': datetime.datetime(2019, 7, 3, 4, 0,
                                  tzinfo=tzutc()),
 'description': '5 qubit device Vigo',
 'dt': 2.2222222222222221e-10,
 'dtm': 2.2222222222222221e-10}
```

The ability to get this information programmatically is particularly useful when finding specific properties across different devices or when collecting data. The following code finds the two qubits with the lowest CNOT error rate between them, out of all the devices from the provider:

```
def find_best_cx(provider):
    """Find the best (lowest error) CXGate
    across all qubits available in `provider`"""

    best_err, best_backend, best_pair = (
        1, None, None)
    for backend in provider.backends():
        conf = backend.configuration()

        # Skip simulators and single-qubit devices
```

```
        if conf.simulator or conf.num_qubits < 2:
          continue

        for pair in conf.coupling_map:
          err = backend.properties().gate_error(
                                        'cx', pair)
          if err < best_err:
            best_err, best_backend, best_pair = (
                err, backend, pair)

    return (best_backend, best_pair, best_err)
```

Finally, we can view and change a backend's default options through the `.options` attribute. This next code block shows the default options for `FakeVigo` (again, with some information omitted):

```
vigo = FakeVigo()
vigo.options

Options(shots=1024, method=None, device='CPU',
precision='double', seed_simulator=None, ...,
mps_omp_threads=1)
```

These are the default values `vigo` will use when running circuits. If we overwrite these (e.g., with `vigo.options.shots = 2048`), this will change the default for this instance of the object, i.e., `vigo.run(qc)` will use the new number of shots. Note that this will not overwrite the default for *other* instances of the object, so running `vigo = FakeVigo()` will reset `vigo.options` to its initial state.

Interacting with Quantum Systems on the Cloud

So far, we've treated remote backends in the same way as local backends, and all the functionality we've seen so far in the chapter applies to both. When using remote backends, however, we will often have to wait for network processes and

---

device queues, which we don't experience with local backends. Qiskit includes some tools to help with this.

Convenience Tools

The job_monitor function regularly checks the status of a job and displays it to the user. If backend is a remote Backend object, and qc is a valid QuantumCircuit, then this code runs the circuit remotely and monitors the job:

```
from qiskit.tools import job_monitor
job = backend.run(qc)
job_monitor(job)
```

As the job progresses, we'll see updates printed, such as the following:

```
Job Status: job is being validated
Job Status: job is queued (1)
Job Status: job is actively running
Job Status: job has successfully run
```

Runtime Services

As we've seen, processing and queueing jobs can add a significant wait time to our experiments. While this is OK for one-off circuit executions, it makes carrying out any experiment that requires feedback loops between circuit creators and circuit results difficult. Variational algorithms (such as the VQE, discussed in Chapter 7) are one such example.

As a solution, providers can offer runtime services that accept inputs for algorithms and that run these algorithms in full (not resubmitting jobs for each circuit execution). For example, the following code defines a VQE algorithm as a dictionary. This includes the problem (the variable op here), and other algorithm parameters. Refer to Chapter 7 for more information on the VQE algorithm:

```
from qiskit.circuit.library import TwoLocal
from qiskit.algorithms.optimizers import COBYLA
from qiskit.opflow import X, Y, Z, I
```

```
op = ( .5 * (X ^ Y ^ Z)
      + .2 * (Y ^ Y ^ I)
      - .3 * (Z ^ X ^ Z)
      + .2 * (I ^ X ^ Y))

runtime_inputs = {
  'ansatz': TwoLocal(3, 'rx', 'cx'),
  'initial_parameters': 'random',
  'operator': op,
  'optimizer': COBYLA(maxiter=500)
}
```

With this procedure defined, we can then send this off to our provider to complete the full algorithm and return the results:

```
from qiskit import IBMQ
provider = IBMQ.load_account()

job = provider.runtime.run(
    program_id='vqe',
    options={
        'backend_name': 'ibmq_qasm_simulator'},
    inputs=runtime_inputs
)

result = job.result()
```

The runtime programs available will depend on your provider.

## CHAPTER 10

OpenQASM

QASM is a low-level, imperative programming language, describing quantum programs in terms of the specific actions the quantum computer should take.

It is an intermediate representation between human-editable descriptions of quantum programs (such as Qiskit's `Quantum Circuit`) and quantum hardware controllers. To enable it to describe full quantum programs, QASM also supports some basic classical logic, similar to higher-level classical languages such as C.

In this chapter, we'll cover only gate-level operations, but QASM does also support some pulse-level quantum programming too.

Building Quantum Circuits in QASM

In this section, we'll cover the QASM syntax needed to create simple quantum circuits.

Comments

Before we start, we'll learn how to annotate the code we're writing.

You can use comments as messages to other humans reading your code (including your future self). Two slashes (//) will mark the rest of the line as a comment. You can also use the character sequences /* and */ to mark the start and end of comments, respectively, over many lines. We'll use comments to describe the code examples in this chapter:

```
The compiler will read this // but not this
/* or any
of this */
```

Version Strings

At the time of writing, there are three versions of QASM, so you might want to specify which version of QASM you're writing in. For this reason, the first noncomment line of a QASM file can be a *version string* (an example follows). In this chapter, all code will be in QASM 3.0, so we will mostly ignore version strings. The version string starts with OPENQASM, followed by a space, the major version, a period, the minor version, and a semicolon. Here is the version string for OpenQASM 3.0, which we use in this chapter:

```
OPENQASM 3.0;
```

Basic Syntax

QASM is a rich language that can describe complex quantum programs, including classical and quantum routines. In this section, we'll ignore most of these features and worry only about creating individual quantum circuits. We'll see how to create more sophisticated programs later on in this chapter.

The quantum systems targeted by QASM can have any number of qubits and may support any kind of quantum gates. In this subsection, we'll imagine a system with three qubits that supports CX gates and U gates. To start, let's look at the QASM code that describes the "hello, world!" of quantum circuits: a circuit that creates a GHZ state, in which our qubits are in an equal superposition of $|000\rangle$ and $|111\rangle$. We'll also add some measurements so our experimentalists can verify this. Figure 10-1 shows the circuit we'll create.

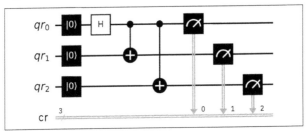

Figure 10-1. A simple quantum circuit

The following QASM code produces the circuit shown in Figure 10-1:

```
// Declare data type[number] name; ❶
qubit[3] qr;
bit[3] cr;

// Initialize qubits to |0> ❷
reset qr[0];
reset qr[1];
reset qr[2];

// Specify quantum gates ❸
h qr[0];
CX qr[0], qr[1];
CX qr[0], qr[2];

// Measure to classical bits ❹
cr[0] = measure qr[0];
cr[1] = measure qr[1];
cr[2] = measure qr[2];
```

❶ First, we declare and name the data (both quantum and classical) that we'll be manipulating. A declaration starts with the type, followed by the name, and ends with a semicolon. The two data types we use here are bit and qubit, two things you should already be familiar with. Like many other programming languages, the square bracket notation allows us to declare an array of a type. In the first noncode line, we're declaring that we'll manipulate three qubits, and in the next two we name the data. We called our array of qubits qr and our array of bits cr. Finally, we end the line with a semicolon.

❷ Next, we initialize each qubit to the state $|0\rangle$ using the reset instruction. Here, we're using the square bracket notation to access the individual elements of the qr array.

❸ We now tell the quantum computer how to manipulate our qubits. As with classical assembly languages, we first specify the operation, then the data we want to apply the operation to. For example, h qr[0]; tells the quantum computer to perform an H gate on the first qubit in the array qr. We end these lines with a semicolon.

❹ Finally, we need to measure our qubits to see the results. The quantum gates we applied before had no "output"; they just changed the state of the qubits. But the measure operation *does* return something (a bit), and we can assign its outputs to our classical bits.

Implicit Looping

When programming, we often find ourselves repeating the same operation on many items. QASM supports syntax to simplify this; if we apply an operation to an array, the compiler will try to repeat this operation on each item in that array. For example, this snippet:

```
qubit[3] qr;
h qr;
```

declares a three-qubit array named qr and applies an H gate to each qubit in qr. This is shorthand for the following:

```
qubit[3] qr;
h qr[0];
```

```
    h qr[1];
    h qr[2];
```

This behavior is the same for all operations that act on a single type. For operations that take two inputs, the operation will try to iterate through any arrays in unison. For example, in the following code, we iterate through two arrays of qubits (named control and target):

```
    qubit[3] control;
    qubit[3] target;

    CX control, target;
```

This produces the circuit shown in Figure 10-2 and is equivalent to the following code:

```
    qubit[3] control;
    qubit[3] target;

    CX control[0], target[0];
    CX control[1], target[1];
    CX control[2], target[2];
```

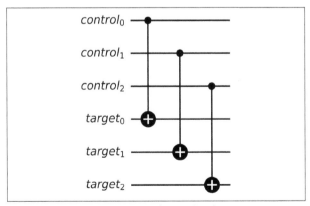

Figure 10-2. A two-register circuit where each qubit in one register is controlled by each qubit in the other

This behavior makes sense only if the two arrays are the same size, so if we apply a multi-input operation on two arrays of different sizes, the compiler will raise an error. If any of the inputs are not arrays, then the compiler will not attempt to iterate through those inputs and will use the same input for each operation in the loop.

For example, in the following code, qr[0] refers to a single qubit (not an array), but qr[1:2] does refer to an array (containing qubits qr[1] and qr[2]):

```
qubit[3] qr;
CX qr[0], qr[1:2];
```

The compiler will repeat the operation for each item in qr[1:2], with the control qubit qr[0]. Figure 10-3 shows the circuit described by the preceding code.

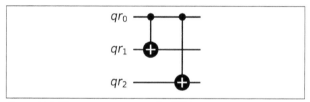

Figure 10-3. The quantum gates in the GHZ circuit

With this new syntax, we can create the GHZ circuit we saw in the previous section with the shorter, more readable, and more flexible code:

```
// Declare data
qubit[3] qr;
bit[3] cr;

// Initialize qubits to |0>
reset qr;

// Specify quantum gates
h qr[0];
CX qr[0], qr[1:2];
```

```
// Measure to classical bits
cr = measure qr;
```

Figure 10-4 shows the circuit produced by this code.

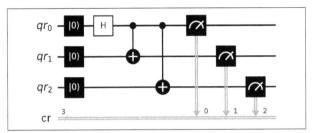

Figure 10-4. A simple quantum circuit

Quantum Gates and Instructions

In this subsection, we'll see how to describe some basic quantum operations through QASM.

Gates

QASM understands two quantum gates out of the box: the single-qubit U gate and the two-qubit CNOT. Together, these two gates are universal, meaning we can build any quantum gate from a combination of these two gates.

The U gate is the most general single-qubit gate. It's a parameterized gate, and we specify the parameters using rounded brackets after the instruction. For example, the following code applies a U gate to the third qubit of the quantum register qr:

```
U(0, 0, pi) qr[3];
```

The definition of the U gate from the OpenQASM specification is the same as the U gate implemented in Qiskit:

$$U(\theta, \phi, \lambda) := \begin{pmatrix} \cos\left(\theta/2\right) & -e^{i\lambda}\sin\left(\theta/2\right) \\ e^{i\phi}\sin\left(\theta/2\right) & e^{i(\phi+\lambda)}\cos\left(\theta/2\right) \end{pmatrix}$$

This definition has three parameters, theta (θ), phi (ϕ), and lambda (λ), and as such, the U command requires these three parameters; i.e., U(theta, phi, lambda).

The other built-in gate is CNOT, which has the command CX.

Instructions

QASM also supports two built-in, nonunitary quantum instructions. The first is reset, which resets a qubit to $|0\rangle$:

```
qubit[4] qr;
reset qr;  // Set all qubits in qr to |0>
```

The second is measure, which measures the state of a qubit in the computational basis (a.k.a. the Z-basis) and writes the result to an output bit. These measurements project the state of a qubit to either $|0\rangle$ or $|1\rangle$, and we can immediately start manipulating this qubit after measurement:

```
bit[3] cr;
qubit[3] qr;
reset qr;

cr = measure qr;
```

Building Higher-Level Gates

In the previous section, we saw the QASM's basic syntax and built-in operations. In this section, we'll look at how we can build custom operations from these built-in commands.

Modifying Existing Gates

One of the ways we can describe more complicated quantum gates is through *gate modifiers*. Wherever we use a quantum gate, we can prefix that gate with a modifier keyword and the @ character to change that gate's behavior.

For example, the ctrl modifier controls a gate on the state of another qubit (active only if the controlling qubit is $|1\rangle$). For example, since U(0, 0, pi) is the Pauli Z gate, the following code performs the controlled-Z gate on the first two qubits of qr:

```
// Controlled-Z gate
ctrl @ U(0, 0, pi) qr[0], qr[1];
```

Figure 10-5 shows the circuit described by the preceding code.

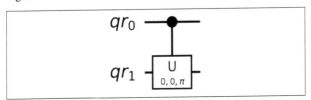

Figure 10-5. A controlled-U gate

Similarly, the negctrl modifier conditions the gate on the state of the control qubit being $|0\rangle$.

The inv modifier *inverts* a gate. For example, in the next code snippet, we apply a T gate to the qubit q, followed by the inverse of the T gate (i.e., the $T^{\dagger}$ gate). This sequence of gates is equivalent to doing nothing (the identity operation):

```
U(0, 0, pi/4) qr;  // T gate
inv @ U(0, 0, pi/4) qr;  // T† gate
```

Figure 10-6 shows the circuit described by the preceding code.

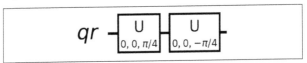

Figure 10-6. A U gate, followed by its inverse

Finally, the pow(n) modifier repeats the gate n times:

```
pow(3) @ U(0, 0, pi/4) qr;
```

Figure 10-7 shows the circuit described by this code.

Figure 10-7. A U gate repeated twice

We can also stack these modifiers as in the following:

```
inv @ pow(3) @ U(0, 0, pi/4) qr;
```

Figure 10-8 shows the circuit described by this code.

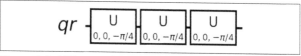

Figure 10-8. A U(0, 0, pi/4) gate, inverted and repeated twice

Defining New Gates

To declare a new quantum gate, we use the `gate` keyword, followed by:

1. The name of the new gate

2. Any parameters the gate takes (in parentheses)

3. Names of qubits the gate acts on

4. The gate's definition in terms of other operations (inside curly brackets)

For example, the following code defines a controlled-RZ gate:

```
// Call gate 'crz'
// Gate takes one parameter (phi)
// Gate acts on two qubits (q0 & q1)
gate crz(phi) q0, q1 {
    ctrl @ U(0, 0, phi) q0, q1;
}
```

The following code shows this gate definition in action; once we've defined a new gate type, we can use it just like any other gate:

```
// Define controlled-RZ gate
gate crz(phi) q0, q1 {
    ctrl @ U(0, 0, phi) q0, q1;
}

// Declare circuit data types
qubit[2] qr;
bit[2] cr;

// Construct simple circuit
reset qr;
crz(pi/4) qr[0], qr[1];
cr = measure qr;
```

The preceding code describes the quantum circuit shown in Figure 10-9.

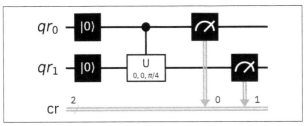

Figure 10-9. A circuit containing resets, a controlled-U operation, and measurements

Classical Types and Instructions

In the previous sections, we used two of the data types that QASM supports. The first is the qubit, the smallest unit of quantum information, and the other is the bit, the smallest unit of classical information. We also saw that we could declare and operate on *arrays* of those types using the square bracket syntax:

```
bit b0;       // Declare a bit named 'b0'
qubit q0;     // Declare a qubit named 'q0'
bit[2] cr;    // Array of 2 bits named 'cr'
qubit[3] qr;  // Array of 3 qubits named 'qr'
```

Due to the limited nature of near-term devices, the only quantum data type QASM supports is the qubit. However, quantum circuits are controlled by classical routines, and QASM does support many different classical types to make this easier. All classical types in QASM are arrays of bits, but it's much easier to abstract this out a level to types we're more familiar with in higher-level languages.

The syntax is the same as with declaring arrays (i.e., type[size] name). For example, this declares an integer (more on this to come) with 16 bits, named my_int:

```
int[16] my_int;
```

Table 10-1 lists some classical data types available in QASM 3.0.

Table 10-1. Classical data types supported by QASM

Type	Description
bit	We've already seen this type. This is the smallest unit of classical information and can have values of either 0 or 1. All other classical types are built from bits.
int	This data type represents a signed integer (i.e., an integer that can be negative). One of the bits stores the sign (+ or -), and the rest store the integer in binary notation. This means n bits can store integers between -2^{n-1} and 2^{n-1}.
uint	This data type represents *unsigned* (positive) integers. n bits can store integers between 0 and 2^n.
float	This data type uses the IEEE 754 specification to represent floating-point numbers.
angle	You're less likely to have seen this as a built-in data type in other low-level languages, but due to the rotational nature of quantum gates, QASM allows us to specify an *angle* as a fraction of a full rotation. n bits allows us to specify angles between 0 and 2π within an error of $\pm\ 2\pi/2^n$. Casting a different value to an angle takes the remainder of that value after dividing by 2π.

Type	Description
complex	This data type represents a complex number. We can build this type from either two ints or two floats of equal size, depending on the precision you want. This means we pass either an int or a float as the size (e.g., complex[int[32]] name;). The keyword im represents the complex unit $i = \sqrt{-1}$.
bool	Like the bit, this type can take one of two values, in this case true or false.

Constants

We can declare constant (immutable) classical types using the const keyword:

```
const uint[16] x = 44;
```

Shorthands

Some shorthands are useful when declaring classical types:

- When declaring an array of bits, we can use a string of 0 and 1 characters (e.g., bit[10] my_bits = '0011111011';).
- We can use scientific notation to declare large or small numbers (e.g., float[32] name = 2.34e5;).
- QASM supports some popular mathematical constants that we can use to declare types, including the following:
  - When declaring ints and floats, we can use the keywords pi, tau, and euler (e.g., float[32] name = 4*euler;).
  - When declaring a complex type, we can use the im keyword to represent the imaginary unit (e.g., complex[float[32]] my_complex = 3.1 + 1.2im;).

Arrays of Classical Types

We've already seen how to create arrays of bits and qubits with the square bracket syntax:

```
qubit[3] qr;   // Array of 3 qubits
bit[3] cr;     // Array of 3 bits
```

But we can also create arrays of the higher-level classical types through the array keyword. This keyword should be followed by the type and the size of the array in square brackets. For example, the following code creates an array of 10 16-bit ints, named int_array:

```
array[int[16], 10] int_array;
```

And we can access each element of int_array using square brackets as we did with bit and qubit arrays. We can also specify all the values of an array when declaring it using curly brackets:

```
array[float[64], 3] my_array = {0.1, 2.9, pi};
```

QASM also supports multidimensional arrays; we just need to pass the extra dimension to the array constructor. In the code that follows, we create a 2D array of 32-bit units, named matrix:

```
// 8x8, 2D array
array[uint[32], 8, 8] matrix;
```

Built-in Classical Instructions

QASM supports some common operations between classical data of the same type. All instructions shown here must have a data type on the left-hand side (LHS) of the instruction and a value of the same type on the right-hand side (RHS). For example, the assignment operator (=) sets the value of the data on the LHS to the value on the RHS:

```
bit x;   // Declare bit
x = 1;   // Set x to 1
```

All data types except `complex` support the comparison operators shown in Table 10-2.

Table 10-2. Classical comparisons supported by QASM

Name	Symbol	Description
Equal to	==	Compares the value on the RHS to the value on the LHS and returns True if, and only if, both sides are equal
Not equal to	!=	Returns False if, and only if, both sides are equal
Less than	<	Returns True if LHS is less than RHS
Greater than	>	Returns True if LHS is greater than RHS
Less than or equal to	<=	Returns True if LHS is less than or equal to RHS
Greater than or equal to	>=	Returns True if LHS is greater than or equal to RHS

All numeric types (`int`, `float`, `angle`, and `complex`) support the basic arithmetic operations in Table 10-3.

Table 10-3. Classical numeric instructions supported by QASM

Name	Symbol	Description
Addition	+	Returns value of LHS added to RHS
Multiplication	*	Returns value of LHS multiplied by RHS
Power	**	Returns value of LHS to the power (exponent) of RHS
Division	/	Returns value of LHS divided by RHS (note that dividing two `int`s returns an `int`)

Along with the operations in Table 10-3, integers (`int`) also support the modulo operation shown in Table 10-4.

Table 10-4. Classical integer instructions supported by QASM

Name	Symbol	Description
Modulo	%	Returns the value of LHS modulo RHS (i.e., the remainder of LHS divided by RHS)

As with most programming languages, we can also condition operations on the state of a bool and the if keyword. The if keyword must be followed by the bool (in parentheses), then by the conditioned logic (in curly brackets). We can then follow this with the else keyword to trigger instructions only if the statement was false. For example, this code calculates the maximum value of a and b and stores it in c:

```
if (a < b) {
    c = b;
} else {
    c = a;
};
```

With this classical logic, we can now encode more complicated quantum circuits, such as the famous quantum teleportation circuit shown in Figure 10-10.

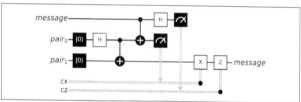

Figure 10-10. The quantum teleportation protocol

The following QASM code encodes the teleportation algorithm shown in Figure 10-10:

```
// Declare two bits to be transmitted
bit cz;
bit cx;

// Declare message and entangled pair
qubit message;
qubit[2] pair;

// Third party entangles pair
h pair[0];
cx pair[0], pair[1];
```

```
// Third party gives pair[0] to message sender
// and pair[1] to message recipient

// Message sender then entangles pair[0] with
// the message qubit, and measures
cx message, pair[0];
h message;
cz = measure message;
cx = measure pair[0];

// Message sender sends two classical bits to
// message recipient
if (cx == 1) {
    x pair[1];
}

if (cz == 1) {
    z pair[1];
}
```

QASM supports while loops, which repeat instructions as long as a condition is true. For example, the following snippet implements an inefficient way of resetting a qubit (q) to $|0\rangle$:

```
qubit q;
bit b = 1;

while (b==1) {
    h q;
    b = measure q;
}
```

QASM also supports for loops, which repeat instructions for each item in an array. For example, this code block applies an H gate to each qubit in qr:

```
qubit[3] qr;

for q in qr {
    h q;
}
```

Building Quantum Programs

We have now covered everything needed to create rich, circuit-level quantum programs in QASM. In this section, we'll look at two QASM features that make managing and reusing programs easier.

Subroutines

Similar to custom gate definitions, we can combine both classical and quantum instructions into a *subroutine*. A subroutine definition starts with the def keyword, followed by the name of the subroutine. Next, we declare and name the data types the subroutine will act on (in parentheses), then indicate the data type that the subroutine returns (after a -> symbol). The subroutine instructions follow, enclosed by curly brackets.

To illustrate, the following code creates a subroutine named bell_measurement that measures two qubits in the Bell basis. This subroutine takes an array of two qubits and returns two bits:

```
def bell_measure(qubit[2] qr) -> bit[2] {
    CX qr[0], qr[1];
    h qr[0];
    return measure qr;
}
```

To use this subroutine in a program, we follow the subroutine's name with the arguments, enclosed in parentheses:

```
qubit[2] qr;
bit[2] cr;

cr = bell_measure(qr);
```

Note that you can declare classical data types in the body of a subroutine but not quantum data types.

Inputs and Outputs

We've seen that instructions and subroutines can accept inputs and return outputs, and this is also true of entire QASM programs; when we declare classical data, we can prefix the declaration with the `input` keyword, which means the value of that data will only be known at runtime. In the following code, we declare an array of 20 `angles` named `point` and tell QASM that this value will be known only at runtime:

```
input angle[20] point;
```

By leaving some values unknown when compiling, we can avoid repeating long compilation and optimization processes. This is especially useful for near-term, variational algorithms that require many circuit runs with different gate parameters.

We can also specify any classical data types that our program should output using the `output` keyword. If we don't specify any outputs, then the QASM program will output *all* classical data.

Index

About the Authors

James L. Weaver is a developer, author, and speaker with a passion for quantum computing. He is a Java Champion and a JavaOne Rockstar. James has written books including *Inside Java* (Addison-Wesley), *Beginning J2EE* (Apress), the *Pro JavaFX* series (Apress), and *Java with Raspberry Pi* (Oracle Press). As an IBM Quantum Developer Advocate, James speaks internationally about quantum computing with Qiskit at quantum and classical computing conferences.

Frank J. Harkins is a developer and writer from the north of England. He graduated with a physics degree from the University of Leeds in 2018 and currently works for the Qiskit community team, creating tools for anyone teaching or learning about quantum computing. Frank plays the guitar and enjoys the outdoors.

Colophon

The bird on the cover of *Qiskit Pocket Guide* is a rock bush quail (*Perdicula argoondah*), short-tailed game birds from the shrubland, grassland, and rocky bush of western India. Rock bush quail measure around 7 inches long and weigh around 2.5 ounces. They have barred and mottled brown feathers, gray bills, and orange legs. Their distinctive trilling call rises in pitch and volume.

The rock quail population is decreasing, but the IUCN Red List rates the species as Least Concern. Many of the animals on O'Reilly's covers are endangered; all of them are important to the world.

The cover illustration is by Karen Montgomery, based on a black and white engraving from *English Cyclopedia*. The cover fonts are Gilroy Semibold and Guardian Sans. The text font is Adobe Minion Pro; the heading font is Adobe Myriad Condensed; and the code font is Dalton Maag's Ubuntu Mono.

Milton Keynes UK
Ingram Content Group UK Ltd.
UKHW021123210924
448582UK00010B/142